BECOME A TRUE AQUARIST!

The complete guide to the freshwater aquarium

by

"Mejor Acuario"

2nd Edition. Updated 2023.

Extended Version. English.

Copyright January 2021. Author: Alejandro Sánchez Martínez. All rights reserved.

It is illegal to reproduce, copy or disseminate any part of this document in digital or paper format. Registration of this publication is strictly prohibited.

ISBN: 9798864471241

ACKNOWLEDGMENTS

It has been more than a decade since I became interested in aquariums. These last years I have dedicated my free time to help other colleagues to start their projects and solve their problems.

My thanks to more than 50 people who at some point asked for help, because thanks to you it has been possible to gather the knowledge that is in this book and that now I can and want to share with everyone to whom it may be useful. Project by project we have been adapting and perfecting the equipment and technique until we have found simple guidelines that are applicable and serve as a guide for all our projects.

Thanks to the collaborators who, to a greater or lesser extent, have contributed to the creation of "Better Aquarium": the website, the book, the social networks, etc. To the colleagues whose videos have been mentioned, for allowing me to expand the information and publicize the content of their channels. And also, to "Aquarium Centrofama" that has collaborated in the correction of the manuscript for the 2nd Edition.

The writing of this book has not been an easy task and at times I have been on the verge of quitting. I could not have done it without the support of my family, especially my partner Marta, Lola, my mother and my sister Alicia.

On Facebook: https://www.facebook.com/Mejor-Acuario-100153475359250
And on Instagram: https://www.instagram.com/mejor_acuario/

If you enjoyed the book, please share your experience by leaving a positive comment on Amazon! Your opinion is crucial to us and to other aquarium enthusiasts. Thank you for being a part of our community!

TABLE OF CONTENTS

ACKNOWLEDGMENTS 3
INTRODUCTION 11

PART 1 14

1 THE TANK 16
    1.1   GENERAL RECOMMENDATIONS FOR YOUR CHOICE................................ 16
- Tank shape 17

    1.2   WHAT IS THE RIGHT VOLUME?.. 17
- Why do we recommend a first tank between 70 and 150 liters? 17

    1.3   TYPES OF PROJECTS.. 18
    1.4   WHAT ARE THE IDEAL DIMENSIONS?.. 18
    1.5   HOW MANY LITERS IS YOUR TANK?... 19
    1.6   CHARACTERISTICS OF AQUARIUMS ACCORDING TO THEIR SIZE............ 19
    1.7   THE SIZE OF THE BALLOT BOX AND THE NUMBER OF FISH 20
    1.8   COVERED OR UNCOVERED AQUARIUM.. 20
- How to prevent fish from jumping out of the water?........................ 21

    1.9   BUY A COMPLETE AQUARIUM KIT?... 22
- Some more advantages of choosing your own equipment................. 22

    1.10   WHERE TO BUY YOUR AQUARIUM TANK?... 23
- Find a new tank... 23
- Find a used tank.. 23

2 WHERE TO PUT THE AQUARIUM?.. 26
    2.1.   CHOOSE A RESISTANT SUPPORT... 26
        2.2   SPECIFIC AQUARIUMS TABLES... 28
- General recommendations for the purchase of specific tables.......... 29

    2.3   TIPS FOR CHOOSING THE RIGHT SITE.. 30

3 THE FILTER 35

- 3.1 THE TWO MOST IMPORTANT FEATURES OF THE FILTER 35
  - Is flow rate or capacity more important? 36
- 3.2 HOW DOES A FILTER WORK? 37
  - Direction of water flow and placement of filter media 38
- 3.3 TYPES OF FILTERS 38
- 3.4 OTHER ASPECTS OF CHOOSING THE FILTER FOR YOUR PROJECT 41
- 3.5 WHAT CAPACITY AND FLOW RATE SHOULD YOUR FILTER HAVE? 44
  - General recommendations 44
  - Special recommendations 44
  - Our personal recommendation: Oversize the filtration equipment. 44
- 3.6 TWO EXAMPLES OF RECOMMENDED FILTERS 45
  - External filter: eheim pro 46
  - Backpack filter: Seachem tidal 47
  - WHAT ABOUT INTERNAL FILTERS? 49

4 THE FILTER MATERIAL 51

- 4.1 MECHANICAL FILTRATION 51
  - To use or not to use mechanical filter media? 52
  - What mechanical filter media do you need and where to buy it? 53
- 4.2 BIOLOGICAL FILTRATION 54
  - What biological filter media do you need and where to buy it? 54
- 4.3 CHEMICAL FILTRATION 55
  - Some possible uses of chemical filtration 55
  - What chemical filter media do you need and where to buy it? 56
  - Why not to use chemical filter media widely? 56
- 4.4 FILTER MEDIA: KEY IDEAS 56
- 4.5 HOW TO PLACE THE FILTER MEDIA INSIDE THE FILTER? 57
  - Direction of water flow 57

5 HOW TO SET UP THE FILTER 59

- 5.1 HOW TO SET UP AN EXTERNAL FILTER 59
- 5.2 HOW TO ASSEMBLE A BACKPACK FILTER 60
- 5.3 HOW TO SET UP AN INTERNAL FILTER 61
- 5.4 THE MOST IMPORTANT IDEA ABOUT THE FILTERING MATERIAL 61

6 AQUARIUM LIGHTING 63
6.1   GENERAL TIPS FOR LIGHTING YOUR AQUARIUM: 63
6.2   WHAT IS THE IDEAL LAMP FOR YOUR PROJECT? 64

7 THE SUBSTRATE. GRAVELS, SANDS AND NUTRITIVE SUBSTRATES 67
7.1   GENERAL CHARACTERISTICS OF A GOOD SUBSTRATE 67
7.2   RECOMMENDATIONS ACCORDING TO YOUR PARTICULAR PROJECT 68
- Unplanted, with few plants or with less economic investment 68
- Planted aquariums, with greater economic investment 70
- Planted aquariums, economical, but with higher risk 74
- Remenber the key point about the substrate 76

7.3   HOW MANY LITERS OF SUBSTRATE DO I NEED FOR MY AQUARIUM? 77

8 SUMMARY: THE EQUIPMENT YOUR ECOSYSTEM REQUIRES 79
8.1   WHAT DON´T YOU NEED FOR YOUR AQUARIUM? 80

PART 2 82

9 THE IMPORTANCE OF WATER 83
- Diagram of causes and consequences of the quality of our aquarium water 83

9.1   WATER PARAMETERS: GH, KH AND PH 87
- Concepts: GH, KH and pH. 87
- Ideal GH, KH and ph parameters? 88
- How to choose ideal parameters for your specific aquarium? 88

9.2   WATER PARAMETERS: FORGET GH, KH AND PH 89
- How to choose the ppm value for your aquarium water changes? 89
- How to adjust the ppm in the aquarium? 90
- Recommendations for adjusting the ppm of your aquarium water 92
- Other tips 93
- Key ideas on GH, KH and pH 93

9.3   ONE MORE THING BEFORE ADDING WATER TO YOUR AQUARIUM 93

- Water conditioner 93
- 9.4 WATER PARAMETERS: TEMPERATURE ADJUSTMENT 94
  - Thermometer 95
  - Aquarium heater - Do I need a heater for my aquarium? 95
  - How to lower the temperature of my aquarium in summer? The fan 96
  - How to add water to the aquarium when it has evaporated? 97
- 9.5 WATER PARAMETERS: DISSOLVED OXYGEN AND CARBON DIOXIDE 97
  - Factors that decrease O2 and/or increase CO2 in your aquarium 97
  - How to improve gas exchange and dissolved oxygen in water? 98
- 9.6 WATER PARAMETERS: AMMONIUM, NITRITES, NITRATES AND OTHER 100
  - What is the nitrogen cycle? 100
  - What is aquarium cycling? 102
  - General information on cycling 102
  - How to cycle? 103
  - How to accelerate aquarium cycling? 104
  - How to introduce the first fish into the aquarium? 106
  - Recommendations to consider during cycling 107
  - What to do when the cycling is over? 108
- 9.7 WATER: LASTEST TIPS 108
  - Measures to reduce metal toxicity 108

10 AQUARIUM AUTOMATION, MAINTENANCE AND CARE 111

- 10.1 USE TIMERS: AUTOMATE WHAT CAN BE AUTOMATED 111
- 10.2 DAILY AQUARIUM CARE 112
- 10.3 WEEKLY AQUARIUM CARE 113
- 10.4 OTHER CARE 113
- 10.5 WATER CHANGES 115
  - How are they made? 115
  - How often should water changes be done? 115
  - Factors decreasing the frequency of water changes 116
- 10.6 HOW TO SIPHON THE AQUARIUM? 116
- 10.7 HOW OFTEN AND HOW DO I CLEAN THE AQUARIUM FILTER? 117
  - Factors extending filter cleaning periods 117

11 DECORATION 119
11.1 GENERAL TIPS FOR DECORATION..121

12 PLANTED AQUARIUM.. 123
12.1 TYPES OF PLANTED AQUARIUM 124
- Low or medium-tech aquariums 124
12.2 BASICS FOR SETTING UP A LOW-MEDIUM TECH AQUARIUM....................129

13 THE END OF ALGAE 132
13.1 COMMON METHODS TO COMBAT AND CONTROL ALGAE 132
13.2 COMPETITION BETWEEN ALGAE AND PLANTS.......................................133
13.3 FACTORS INFLUENCING ALGAE CONTROL...134

14 AQUARIUM INHABITANTS 137
14.1 HOW TO CHOOSE THE SPECIES AND NUMBER OF FISH? 138
- How to research fish species from the start? 138
- Most relevant aspects of each fish species 138
14.2 HOW MANY FISH CAN YOU HAVE ACCORDING TO THE SIZE OF YOUR TANK?..........139
- Factors to consider 139
- Where to get your fish? 140

APPENDIX 1. CHEMICAL FILTRATION 143
APPLICATIONS OF CHEMICAL FILTRATION...143
SOME CHEMICALS FILTER MEDIA..143
- Synthetic adsorbent resins 144
AN EXAMPLE OF HOW TO USE CHEMICAL FILTRATION................................145
THE FOURTH METHOD FOR LOWERING NITRATES.......................................146

APPENDIX 2. EXAMPLES AND BUDGETS OF COMPLETE EQUIPMENT 148
EXAMPLE 1. "THE GOLDFISH TANK"...148
- Essential and recommended equipment 149
EXAMPLE 2. "MY WATER GARDEN"..153
- Essential and recommended equipment 154

INTRODUCTION

First of all, we want to thank you for deciding to get this book. It is a great opportunity for us to share our knowledge and experiences and we are convinced that you will find it really useful.

All of us who have started in the aquarium hobby without a good guide, have bought unnecessary products and inadequate or poor-quality equipment. In addition, without the necessary knowledge, we have made one mistake after another. As a consequence of these bad decisions, problems arise in our aquariums, demotivating many companions who have ended up leaving the hobby. But don't worry, because with this book you will learn, in the easiest, most economical way and in the shortest time possible, how to create a project from scratch and maintain it in excellent conditions.

What is an aquarium? An aquarium is an imitation of nature. You are creating an ecosystem, which must have the ideal conditions for the life of the living beings that inhabit it; this is the **main objective of the book:** *You will be able to create and maintain an ecosystem with the ideal conditions for the life of each of the species of animals and plants that inhabit it. (You will see throughout the book how we use the words aquarium and ecosystem as synonyms).*

The most important part of this ecosystem is the water. Water is to fish as air is to us. If the water is inadequate or polluted, the fish will get sick, suffer and eventually die before they reach their life expectancy. To result in exceptional water for your animals and plants, **your task is simple:** *know and learn to manage the factors that affect and modify the parameters and quality of the water*:

- The filter and filter media.
- Water temperature, hardness, pH...
- Decomposing organic matter and the nitrogen cycle.
- Gases dissolved in water.
- Cleaning and other care.
- Etc.

Understanding how it works and how to manage the ecosystem will be developed mainly in the second part of the book. But just as important is choosing the right equipment:

The filter, the filter material, the substrate, the lighting... and even a pump to make bubbles, are part of and will influence the ecosystem. In the first part of the book, you will learn how to choose one by one all the components of your aquarium. Although we recommend that, if you do not have the equipment yet, do not buy anything until you have finished reading the two parts of this book; this way, you will have seen all the options and you will be able to decide what your project is and how to choose the equipment to carry it out.

Let's not forget that our animals and plants are living beings, that they had a natural habitat, and that once people have taken them out of their habitat, their lives depend on us. We believe that having an aquarium at home is also a small commitment. It is up to each one of us to respect the lives of our animals and plants.

It is not uncommon, for both beginners and those who have been in the hobby for years, to have recurring problems in their ecosystems: their fish get sick, their plants die, their water is cloudy and full of algae, and so on. By the time you finish reading this book, you may not fully understand the mechanisms by which each specific problem develops, nor can colleagues who are considered experts in the hobby often pinpoint it with certainty. But it doesn't matter, because this is not the key to the solution.

There are many variables and many possible causes and consequences of a problem. If you follow the tips we offer here, **you will learn to master the factors that change the parameters and quality of your water**. In this way, you will probably never have to deal with any of these problems. And if you do, you will know what **the** solution is without knowing for sure what triggered it. ***The ultimate solution to the problems is to*** *correct the factors (filtration, temperature, GH, cleaning of waste products...) that we have neglected to restore the balance.*

A healthy and balanced ecosystem results, with proper care, in healthy fish. They are more resistant to parasites, bacteria, fungi, digestive problems and any other type of acquired disease. And they will fulfill their life expectancy until they die of other natural causes, such as aging, neoplasms, genetic diseases or other problems that are beyond our reach.

In the same way and simultaneously, with the control of these factors (filtration, maintenance, water parameters...) we will be reducing the probability of algae proliferation, the water will be crystal clear (a balanced and stable aquarium does not have cloudy water) and our plants, if we provide them with the care they require, will have no problem to develop and also be part of our ecosystem.

There are many types of ecosystems that we can imitate in our aquariums. With this book you will learn how to create freshwater aquariums, both "cold water" and "warm or tropical water" with all kinds of animals and plants. And we will give you the pillars to support your current project and all your future projects, allowing you to adapt your ecosystem to almost any species of animal or plant, offering you also the possibility to easily create a "biotope" (a faithful recreation of a specific aquatic ecosystem).

In addition to the quality of the water, for your animals to reach their maximum level of well-being, you must know that each species needs specific care and conditions: the ideal size of the tank, the ideal decoration, the hardness of the water, the compatibility between species, the feeding, etc. varies from one species to another. It is important, necessary **and easy to** know the needs of our animal and plant species. And we have two options: to adapt the aquarium to the species we like, or to choose the species according to the characteristics of our aquarium. We will show you how to do it.

An aquarium is something personal, some have plants and others don't, some like shrimp tanks, others like community aquariums and others love salamanders. **Some aquariums require more time of dedication, more care and a greater economic investment and others less.** To enjoy the hobby to the fullest, the latter should be in accordance with your personal situation and your current desires. *We will help you choose the project that best suits you.*

If we take care of our ecosystem, our animals and plants will enjoy good health and this will be reflected in ourselves. This hobby can become your personal refuge. It can be an opportunity to create a place to reflect and see your problems from another perspective.

PART 1

"AQUARIUM EQUIPMENT"

Let's get started!

Although the first part is entitled "Equipment" and focuses on the materials and products we need, aspects of "technique" will also appear, understanding this as "the aquarist's ability to manage the parameters of his ecosystem and to achieve and maintain a water quality suitable for the life of animals and plants".

The aim of this first part is that you will be able to set up an aquarium from scratch, selecting the products you need from all the available options. Whether you are just starting out in the world of aquarium keeping, or you have been doing it for a few years, it will be useful for you.

We also want you to reach the end of the book with an understanding of the most common problems you will face. These are often caused by inadequate equipment and/or poor aquarium management. The solutions will be developed in both the first and second parts of the book. Therefore, even if you read them in greater or lesser detail, we recommend that you do not overlook entire chapters.

Keep in mind that the aquarium is a relatively complex ecosystem, that many variables are involved (light, plants, filtration, species and number of fish and other animals, plants or not, type of substrate, fertilizers, microorganisms, chemical additives...) and that cases like the following are frequent:

José Luis wrote to us about an algae problem in his last project:

A planted aquarium of 70 liters, illuminated with a LED light of about 30 watts and 6000 lumens. A backpack filter of suitable characteristics for those 70 liters, loaded with biological filtration and foam sponge. Gravel as substrate. Fertilized with potassium and weekly water changes of 30%. About 35 fish, which were mostly guppies.

The problem: *Jose, had been having an explosion of green filamentous algae for months and it was getting worse every day. Similar to what we see in this image:*

He explained that he had tried everything, with water changes every 2 days up to 50%, hydrogen peroxide, glutaraldehyde, pruning the most affected leaves and reducing the photoperiod. I had bought some nitrate and phosphate tests, which were 0 with the water changes I was doing. The algae problem was improving, but as soon as I increased the hours of light and went back to weekly water changes, the algae reappeared even with nitrate and phosphate parameters close to 0.

The solution: *change the biological filter material (which was more than 5 years old). Reduce the aquarium population: the number of fish was excessive for such an aquarium and you would have to consider finding a new home for some of them.* **And finally, and probably the most important measure, find plant species that would adapt and grow well in your aquarium.** *Above all, inexpensive, easy to maintain and fast-growing plants (floating plants, "foxtail", "ambulia" and "elodea" are some examples).*

Why? *Overcrowding of the aquarium, coupled with filter media that had exceeded its useful life and slow-growing plants that did not adapt well to the aquarium conditions favored excess nutrients (nitrates, phosphates and others) in the water, which led to rapid algae growth.* **The healthy growth of our plants can purify the water (consuming nutrients to grow), protect our animals and control algae growth.**

If you haven't understood the content, don't worry, you will understand it throughout the book.

Let's get started!

WHAT IS THE FIRST THING YOU SHOULD CHOOSE?

The tank, filter and lighting.

1 THE TANK

This is the container that will hold the water, rocks, logs, plants, substrate, fish, etc. The aquarium has to be adequate to your budget, but also be of quality.

We cannot set up an aquarium with just any tank, due to the risk of water leaks from cracks, breaks or poor sealing of the silicone.

There are many aquarium tanks available on the market. **A quality aquarium, new, in Spain, can be found from 80 euros per 100 liters.**

What is optical glass? It is a glass of greater transparency, close to 100%, which improves the sharpness with which we will see through it. On the downside, it is a bit more expensive and scratches more easily. There are companies in Spain and probably also in the country from which you are reading where you can order customized aquariums, choosing for example that only the front glass of the aquarium is optical and a specific size for the tank.

What is an acrylic aquarium? They are made of a type of plastic. Their advantages are that they are lighter and can be molded in many ways. On the downside, they lose transparency over the years and are more easily scratched. They are also usually more expensive.

1.1 GENERAL RECOMMENDATIONS FOR YOUR CHOICE

- **The cabinet.** The larger the volume in liters you have, the more difficult it is to find a piece of furniture at home that can support the weight of the aquarium. From 90 liters (even less) you should consider the need to buy a specific aquarium cabinet. Our recommendation, if you can afford it, is to buy a specific cabinet.
- **The budget.** The price of equipping (filter, lighting...) a 100-liter tank compared to a 200-liter tank is approximately double (for similar projects where the only variable that changes is the volume of the tank).

Better to have a relatively small aquarium, properly equipped, than to have a large, poorly equipped aquarium.

- **The volume of the tank.** If it is your first aquarium, a tank between 70 and 150 liters may be the most suitable (if you want a larger aquarium, or a smaller one, of course, there is no problem). A little further on we will explain the reason for this recommendation.
- **The shape of the tank.** We recommend that you choose a rectangular or square tank. They are space optimized and fully utilized.

TANK SHAPE

- **Panoramic**: Rectangular with curved front glass. Slightly deform the image of the interior.
- **Spherical** (glass balls). Unpractical, space is not well used and many liters are lost. You would need a very large sphere to have a 40–50-liter aquarium with this shape. In addition, the spherical tank has hardly any oxygen exchange surface between water and air.
- **Cylindrical**: It depends on taste and location. It could be the center of a room.
- **Semi-cylindrical:** They have a half-cylinder shape. The image is deformed and less space is used, but it could be an option to consider depending on its future location.
- **Corner.** They are arranged in a triangular shape covering a corner.

1.2 WHAT IS THE RIGHT VOLUME?

As we said, the first thing to consider will be the space we have at home (or the place where we want to have the tank) and the budget. The more liters you have, the more difficult it is that one of our furniture can support the weight of the aquarium. From 90-100 liters a specific furniture for aquariums is highly recommended.

On the other hand, we also recommend that, if (when you finish reading the book) you are still not clear about the project you want to create, you start by choosing the size of the tank. A volume between 70 and 150 liters allows you a wide variety of projects, at a reasonable price and with relatively little maintenance work.

For an aesthetic reason, the size of the room where the aquarium will be located is also important. For example, if someone has a 40 square meter living room, a 50-liter aquarium is likely to be less visible. On the other hand, a 400-liter aquarium might be excessive in a small room. This question is very personal and depends on each case. With a tape measure you could visualize the aquarium and get an idea of the ideal dimensions you need in your case.

WHY DO WE RECOMMEND A FIRST TANK BETWEEN 70 AND 150 LITERS?

<u>Firstly</u>, because of the difficulty in managing ecosystem parameters. Variations in temperature and other water parameters, increased concentrations of toxic substances (such as ammonium from fish feces and other decomposing organic matter), among other processes, occur more slowly when the aquarium has a larger volume of water. In other words, the larger the volume of water, the more stable the aquarium ecosystem is. **These benefits will not be as relevant after 100 liters of water.**

<u>Secondly</u>, the higher the volume, the higher the economic costs and **maintenance time**.

Finally, volumes between 70 and 150 liters allow a wide variety of projects. The more liters our tank has, in general, the greater the possibilities, since there are species of fish that, due to their size, need tanks of larger volumes. In any case, each project has its own range of recommended volumes.

1.3 TYPES OF PROJECTS

This is not a book to learn how to specifically set up a biotope aquarium, but to discover the basics of any type of aquarium. We can classify them in two types:

- **Common, shared or community aquarium:** A varied number of species of fish, invertebrates and plants will coexist in this aquarium. It is important to keep in mind that not all species of plants and animals can coexist in the same aquarium. Later we will see how to check if they are compatible. We can find them both in amateurs who are just starting out and in those who have been dedicated for years.
- **Biotope aquarium:** these aquariums reproduce the general conditions of a specific tropical region, respecting the water composition, temperature and plant varieties in order to keep fish and other animals native to that region. It is possible to be even more precise with aquariums that reproduce a very specific area of a river ecosystem, for example. These types of aquariums also offer great satisfaction and allow the fish to freely express their natural behaviors. This type of aquarium can also be classified into the following type.
- **Aquascaping aquarium:** this is the art and technique of aesthetically combining stones, rocks, plants, wood, fish and other animals inside an aquarium. The aquascaping designs present different styles, such as the Dutch style aquariums (planted like a garden) or the Japanese style aquariums inspired by nature (such as the Iwagumi style or naturalistic landscaping). There are also others such as: jungle style, biotope aquariums (which would also be a type of landscaping), paludariums and, in the case of saltwater aquariums, saltwater reefs.

1.4 WHAT ARE THE IDEAL DIMENSIONS?

- **Length.** It depends mainly on the space you have and the project you want to carry out. But also, on the budget and the time you can invest in the aquarium, the longer, the more volume and more costs and maintenance time.

- **Height.** It should be in accordance with the length and width (for aesthetic reasons). Also, the higher the height, the more pressure the water exerts; you will need a thicker glass.

    If you are going to have plants, keep in mind that light loses intensity with depth, so you will need a greater investment in lighting. For convenience of maintenance and to avoid problems of poor lighting in aquariums with plants, we do not recommend setting up planted aquariums in tanks over 50-60 cm high.
    It should also be noted that low altitude may limit the mobility of some fish species such as "Pterophyllum scalare" (scalar fish).

    Finally, tall and narrow aquariums offer less surface area contact with the air than wide and low tanks. **Why is this important?** The water surface is where gas exchange occurs, oxygen enters the water and CO_2 escapes. A tank with less exposed water surface favors the need for additional equipment to ensure that your ecosystem receives sufficient oxygen. In any case, the solution to this possible problem is simple, it will be enough to put an air pump (we will see it later).

- **Width.** The wider the width, the more possibilities to "play" with space and planes. Looking at the aquarium through the front glass produces an effect that makes the depth seem shallower than it really is. From 30-35 cm would be an optimal width. For rectangular aquariums we recommend for aesthetic and functional reasons that the width is at least half the length (although it can be very variable depending on the type of project).

1.5 HOW MANY LITERS IS YOUR TANK?

> **Volume** (in liters) = length (cm.) **x** height (cm.) **x** depth (cm.) **/** 1.000
>
> Example: A tank of 100 cm **x** 50 cm **x** 40 cm = 200 liters

1.6 CHARACTERISTICS OF AQUARIUMS ACCORDING TO THEIR SIZE

This classification according to size does not exist as such, we have created it for you for didactic purposes.

- **Nano aquariums up to 10 liters.** Very low light requirement. Very small investment. Unstable aquariums, not recommended for beginners.

- **Small aquariums 10 - 60 liters.** Internal or backpack filter, low light requirement. Low investment. Unstable aquariums. For projects similar to nano aquariums, being able to include species of a larger size than in the previous case.

    Small and **nano aquariums** (from 5 to 50 or 60 liters) are somewhat more complex to operate than medium-sized aquariums. It may seem a contradiction, but the truth is that the smaller an aquarium is, the faster changes in water parameters occur and the more difficult it is to manage.

    For this reason, they are not usually recommended for beginner aquarists. In any case, nano aquariums and small aquariums can be ideal for keeping small fish or shrimp. Also, to have a nice and manageable planted, with the advantage of being much cheaper.

- **Aquariums from 60 - 200 liters.** Backpack filter, external "canister" type filter (most recommended) and in some cases internal (not recommended). They require more powerful lighting screens (if you want to have plants in the aquarium). Average investment, from 200 to 1000 euros (depending on the volume of the tank and the type of project. Throughout the first part you will learn how to make a budget. At the end of the book, there are 2 examples. Stable aquariums. Recommended for beginners. In them you can carry out a great variety of different projects.

- **Aquariums of more than 200 liters.** External canister or backpack filter (in exceptional cases and with high probability of needing more than one). Very high investment, especially if you plan to put plants. Stable aquariums. Aquariums of more than 400 - 500 liters are not recommended for beginners, since the maintenance is complicated (among other cares, if we make weekly water changes of 20-30% of the total volume of an aquarium of 400 liters, it would be 80-100 liters per week).

1.7 THE SIZE OF THE TANK AND THE NUMBER OF FISH

How many fish and what species can I put in my aquarium? We put this topic in this chapter because a very frequent question when we decide to set up our first aquarium: how many fish can I put in the aquarium? There are two ways to approach this question:

1. **Set up a specific or biotope aquarium:** You like a specific species or group of fish species and you want to set up an aquarium for them. For example, you want to set up a Lake Tanganyika biotope aquarium: you will need a minimum volume of 120-200 liters to **fit the adult size of the** species you want to include.

2. **Choosing the right species for your ideal aquarium: this is the most frequent case for those who are new to aquarium keeping.** You are going to choose the volume of your aquarium, or you have already done so, according to the space available at home, your budget, your time and your personal tastes. The question is: **How to choose the species and decide the number of fish for your aquarium?**

In both cases, **you will find the answer in Chapter 14: "The inhabitants of the aquarium"**.

1.8 COVERED OR UNCOVERED AQUARIUM

This is a question that we also have to ask ourselves from the beginning, because we often make an inappropriate decision due to lack of information. In the case that we have decided to buy a custom-made tank (which is our recommendation and we will see it later) we will have the option to buy or not a lid (the lid has a price of 20-30 euros **more for** a 100 liters aquarium).

In addition, this decision may be a determining factor in NOT buying an aquarium set, as these come with a lamp included in the lid.

A. ADVANTAGES OF THE COVERED AQUARIUM
- **Less water evaporation.** You will have to add water to the aquarium less frequently.
- **It protects it from external agents** such as aerosols, products and other objects that may fall inside.
- **Prevents fish from jumping out of** the aquarium.
- **If you have pets**, it might be the best way to prevent them from entering the aquarium. Especially if you have cats.
- **More stable temperature**. It will conserve the temperature better in winter. This can be a disadvantage in summer, as it will increase the water temperature even more and can endanger the life of fish and plants.

B. ADVANTAGES OF THE UNCOVERED AQUARIUM
- **Improved gas exchange.** Both plants and fish need this gas exchange.

- The heat that accumulates between the lid and the water surface makes it difficult for **floating plants to survive.**
- **Decrease in water temperature** in summer.
- Possibility to **better adapt the equipment** we need and our decoration:
    - The lamp.
    - **A fan** to lower the temperature.
    - We will be able to place **the wiring, water inlet and outlet**.
    - We can keep plants and other decorative elements such as rocks or logs emerged (above the water surface).
    - Etc.

The most common reason we justify the need to cover the aquarium is the problem of fish jumping out of the water. But the truth is that, one of the few real reasons why it could be justified to cover the aquarium, would be to have other pets. **There are also fish species that have a tendency to jump out of the water, in this case, you could use "Jumpguard" netting.**

"A Jumpguard netting"

We recommend, in general, that you leave the lid open or buy a tank with NO lid. All of us who have our aquarium uncovered have had a fish jump out of the water, but with the right water quality, this would be something exceptional. Here are some recommendations that will help you avoid this problem:

HOW TO PREVENT FISH FROM JUMPING OUT OF THE WATER?

The best measure, without a doubt, to prevent fish from jumping out of the tank, is clean water in the best conditions.

- **Facilitate gas exchange between air and water**. Preventing the accumulation of CO_2 in the water and providing a sufficient concentration of O_2:
    - Air compressors can be adapted to create bubbles in the water to improve this exchange.
    - "Breaking" the water surface by raising the filter outlet.
    - If we adapt a fan in summer, it also helps to "break" the water surface (to a lesser extent than raising the filter outlet or with an air compressor).
    - Increasing water temperature decreases dissolved O_2.

- - Plants consume CO2 and produce O2 during the day, but during the night, it is the other way around, they consume O2 and produce CO2.
- Good filtration equipment to **keep toxic concentrations to a minimum**.
- Periodic water changes to remove nitrates (product of organic matter decomposition).
- **Have floating plants** and other hiding places for animals to feel safe.
- **Avoid jumping species**.
- Keep in mind that **the first days of adaptation** are the riskiest ones.
- Use of **Jumpguard**.

In short, having a healthy and balanced ecosystem, with clean water, adequate parameters, good filtration, good gas exchange and compatible fish species will prevent our fish from jumping out of the tank.

Don't worry if it seems like too much information, this is the main theme of this book and we will go through it step by step.

1.9 BUYING A COMPLETE AQUARIUM KIT?

Buying a complete set is also an option for beginners in the aquarium hobby. The most outstanding advantage is that it will save you time when deciding the most important components of your aquarium, since they generally always include: a tank, a filter and a lid with the lamp. They also tend to seem relatively inexpensive, but the truth is that you are NOT paying less for more. Their value for money will probably be less than what you will get if you select your own equipment with our advice.

Also keep in mind that **not all aquarium sets are good**. The part in which, most often, these sets fail is the filter, since sometimes they have an insufficient capacity or flow. If it is the first time you set up an aquarium, whether for yourself, shared with your partner or with your children, and you simply want to do it in a very comfortable and easy way, a set can be an option, as long as you assume the limitations in the variety of projects they offer. You will have to discover them yourself with the information in the book or with the help of a specialist in your aquarium store, as this information does not come in the set box.

Since you have come this far and have trusted us, the option we propose and recommend is: set up a custom aquarium by choosing the components separately. With this guide you will have no problem to get the best components separately, we will show you how to do it.

SOME MORE ADVANTAGES OF CHOOSING YOUR OWN EQUIPMENT

- **Better aesthetics.** The tanks of the sets offer limited options. Some of the variables you can choose from are: color of the silicone, black or transparent. Lid or without lid. With lateral reinforcements, or top, or bottom or without any of them, etc.
- **The possibility to adapt the equipment.** The sets usually include a cover and the lamp in it. This limits your possibilities for adapting water inlets and outlets, wiring, fans, etc.
- **Limitations of the filter and lighting.** You would like to have an aquarium with more fish or with plants that need better lighting. For this you need better filtration and better lighting than what you are getting.

1.10 WHERE TO BUY YOUR AQUARIUM TANK?

Let's see how to buy a tank:

FIND A NEW TANK

The starting point is that you have already decided the measures of your tank according to your project or with the indications we have given you. Now, you will find using the Google search engine (for example) and typing: "buy aquarium tank" all the variety of tanks you want, of all possible brands and almost all sizes and volumes you want, in a lot of different stores. Find the one you like best and fits your budget. There are white or black silicone tanks, with or without reinforcements, with or without optical lenses, with or without lid, and many more options. All these features depend on your personal taste. The most important thing is that it is from a trusted brand or company. You can also go to your trusted aquarium store and buy the one that best suits your needs there.

Our recommendation. Have a little patience, buy your custom-made tank from a specialized company and wait for it to arrive at your home (usually in 3 or 4 weeks) or look for one that really suits your needs in your store. To buy a custom-made tank, find a company in your country and order a custom-made tank: optical or normal glass, color of the silicone, with or without corner reinforcements, with or without lid, etc.

To give you a reference, if you live in Spain: a custom-made aquarium, rectangular, 100 liters volume, made of transparent silicone, with optical front glass and without lid, has a price of 90 euros; 110 euros if we include shipping. If you do not live in Spain, find a custom aquarium company with good references and a competitive offer and buy your aquarium there.

It will be an aquarium to enjoy for at least 10 to 15 years and if we change the silicone after this period of time, to enjoy it for life.

FIND A USED TANK

If you need to find something cheaper. Use a second-hand market and start looking for the aquarium that fits the measurements you want. For example, in Spain: "Milanuncios", "Wallapop" or "Vibbo" could be a good option. Probably these options are also a good choice in your country. "Facebook" is also a good option. There are dozens of groups dedicated to aquatics and in many of these groups buying and selling is allowed. There are even specific groups for second hand aquarium equipment for aquarists.

Another place where we have found good deals and where you can find good recommendations is in "WhatsApp" groups. If you have the opportunity to join a group in or around your area, don't hesitate to do so.

A. RISKS OF A SECOND-HAND TANK

The silicone used to bond the glass in aquariums has a life span of approximately 10-15 years. Therefore, it is very important to know how old the aquarium you are being offered is.

B. TIPS YOU SHOULD KNOW BEFORE YOU BUY

- Ask how old the aquarium is. Remember that silicone has a shelf life of approximately 10 years.
- If you still have the purchase receipt it would be ideal.
- Another necessary question is where the aquarium has been stored and for how long. If it has been in a place with extreme temperatures, the silicone may have been more affected over time and be more at risk of leaking.
- Ask for a video test to verify that the aquarium is not leaking.
- Check with photos or videos that the aquarium is not scratched or cracked.

Once you have been able to check all these actions, it is time to see the aquarium in person.

C. WHAT SHOULD YOU INSPECT IN A USED AQUARIUM?

- You should check that the aquarium is not scratched or cracked.
- If it has cracks, discard it immediately.
- Ensure that the silicone is in good condition, unless you want to buy it at a lower price and are willing to change the silicone.
- Check the corners well.

D. CLEANING A SECOND-HAND AQUARIUM

When you buy a second-hand aquarium, you should clean it yourself thoroughly. For proper cleaning of the aquarium, we recommend using white vinegar. Just pour a little on the lime and let it act for a few minutes. With a kitchen sponge scouring pad **(do not use the aluminum ones)** you can finish removing the remains. You will find videos on "YouTube" that will help you to clear the doubts (always contrast the information you find on the internet).

2 WHERE TO PUT THE AQUARIUM?

The furniture where to put the aquarium depends, normally, on the size of the tank you want to set up, but it can also be the following case: *the aquarium you like has a volume of 200 liters, but at home or in the room where you want to put it you do not have any furniture that can support this weight and you are not willing to buy a specific furniture for aquariums. So finally, you choose a smaller aquarium.*

In which room of the house do you want to put it? Watching fish swim around in your office oblivious to what's going on outside can be enjoyable for many people. An aquarium customized to your taste and with the right color scheme can be the focal point of a room's decor. There are also other aquarists who prefer to reserve specific rooms. They are usually people very dedicated to this hobby, with several aquariums and who also have an aquarium on display in their living room. All of these could be a good option.

Keep in mind that, by placing your aquarium in one of the main rooms of the house, it should look neat and "visible" most of the time, both by potential visitors and by you or your family. It is not nice to have a neglected aquarium in plain sight. It will go from being a "Zen", relaxing or meditative retreat to a corner you will want to avoid looking at.

You could also put it in your workplace or in your company, where your customers can also enjoy it.

2.1. CHOOSE A STURDY SUPPORT

We cannot put a 100-liter tank just anywhere in our house. Keep in mind that one liter of water is equal to approximately one kilogram. We leave you two examples of furniture that you can have at home, with the characteristics that make them suitable or not:

This piece of furniture has a **horizontal wooden surface** about 3 cm thick, approximately 1-meter-long x 60 cm wide, which rests on 3 **perpendicular wooden boards**, 2 on the sides and 1 on the back.

This cabinet is an example that **could hold up to 120-150 liters.**

In contrast, the horizontal surface of this one is thinner, about 2 cm or less. In addition, it is anchored to the wall and without supports perpendicular to the floor. This cabinet would **NOT** be suitable for an aquarium. Even if it is 20 liters or less, we do not recommend using this type of furniture.

Using unsuitable furniture can lead to relatively serious problems. In the second case, we see a piece of furniture that can probably support a tank weighing 20 kilograms. Even so, with the risk that at some point it may come loose, we believe that it is not necessary to assume this kind of risk.

Note also that, because this furniture is not designed to support the weight of an aquarium. It is possible that the table may sink slightly in the center, being definitely deformed (both in the first and in the second example that we have presented above). This will depend on each case; we will show you now:

This table with the legs located at the corners would be an example of a table with a high probability of sinking and deforming slightly in the center.

(This is only an example of a table in which the weight is supported by the ends).

On the other hand, this one, where the weight of the aquarium falls on the main support, will not bend.

*This table is **not** recommended for an aquarium, it has a very high center of gravity (the weight-bearing leg is very high). In addition, it has no lateral supports to give it stability. A blow could make it fall to one of the sides.*

These last two are just examples to help us understand some of the most frequent problems we may have.

On the other hand, there is the problem of humidity. You will have to take special care with humidity in your furniture and tables that are not intended for aquariums, drying quickly the drops that may fall on the wood. Even so, you will have to assume that, in the long run, the wood will eventually deteriorate at a faster rate than usual.

Another important aspect is to make **sure** that **you** do **not have to move the cabinet once the tank is filled** with water.

If you already have a piece of furniture at home that can support the weight, perfect! Use it and skip the next part! And remember that setting up a smaller aquarium is also an option.

But if you don't have a suitable piece of furniture at home: get a specific aquarium stand!

2.2 SPECIFIC AQUARIUMS TABLES

You will find pages where they will recommend you to buy furniture that can be used to put an aquarium, with titles such as: *"The Best Furniture ... for Aquariums!* In Best Aquarium we have reviewed many of these pages, we have personally seen some of these furniture and we have seen the prices of this furniture.

CONCLUSION: If you already have a cabinet, use it. But if you don't, the price difference between a normal, low-quality cabinet and a specific aquarium cabinet can be between 20-40 euros more expensive (if the quality of the cabinet is similar the price will probably be the same). We are talking about a piece of furniture that you will be able to keep for 20 or 30 years (depending on its use). **It is worth paying the small price difference**! and buying a specific aquarium furniture.

WHY?

- They are designed to support the weight.
- They are resistant to humidity.
- They have shelves, recesses and cabinets to store all equipment and wiring.
- They are aesthetic.
- They will last a long time in good condition.
- And the most important thing: *They won't give you troubles!*

Choose the aquarium stand that you like and fits the size of your aquarium.

A. IMAGES OF SPECIFIC AQUARIUM FURNITURE

We leave these images in case you did not know the existence of this kind of furniture. In Google, you will find guides where you can see the characteristics of the different pieces of furniture and choose the one you like the most and adapts to your needs.

Fluval Roma

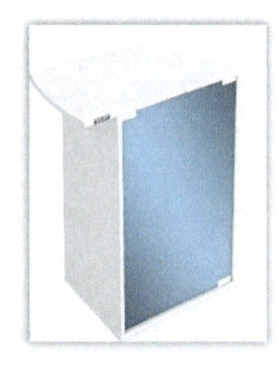

Tetra AquaArt Cabinet

Ciano Emotions Nature Furniture

Juwel Furniture Sbx Lido 120.    *Juwel - Aquarium Cabinet Primo*    *Juwel Furniture SBX Rio 125.*

There are many stores with good offers. Get them at the store you trust that best suits your needs.

GENERAL RECOMMENDATIONS FOR THE PURCHASE OF SPECIFIC TABLES

- Make it a cabinet, with or without shelves, to store inside the filter and the rest of the equipment. If you have it, you could also store the CO2 bottle in the cabinet.
- **The most important thing is to pay attention to the length and width of the surface (the wood on which the aquarium rests).** The tank **must NOT protrude**, not even one centimeter, over the edges of the table because of the risk of breakage.
- If you subtract 5 cm from the total height of each piece of furniture, you can get an idea of the height of the inner cabinet. For example: If the cabinet from the floor to the table is 75 cm, the inner cabinet will be about 70 cm high to store your equipment.
- If you search for your furniture on Amazon, the measurements provided by the website are sometimes incorrect.
- We will not mind if there are a few centimeters of table length left over, for example: a 60 cm long aquarium and a 70 cm long table.
- We recommend that the width is better adjusted for aesthetic reasons. Although it is not essential and later you could adapt a larger tank.
- The liters that you see in the names of the furniture are NOT the maximum liters that the table can support. These pieces of furniture are of brands and are designed for their own aquariums, they refer to the aquarium (of their own brand) for which they were initially designed. We will put the one we want.
- If you Google the word "buy" followed by the name of the furniture you will find several offers. Look for the cheapest and always from reputable companies. You can also find them in some aquarium stores.
- Last and most important: **buy the one you like the most!**

We leave you this example of a tank with its specific furniture:

"An example of a specific aquarium furniture"

2.3 TIPS FOR CHOOSING THE RIGHT SITE

1. **Avoid the sun.** Keep the aquarium away from direct sunlight. It is not a matter of keeping it in a dark room, what happens is that, if the sunlight falls directly on our aquarium, it will facilitate the appearance of algae (especially in non-planted aquariums) and in warm regions it will be difficult to control the water temperature in summer. The sun should not be avoided in all cases, there are hobbyists with planted aquariums that allow direct sunlight to reach their aquariums (not in the hours of highest intensity) and thus can also reduce the light intensity of artificial lighting.

2. **Avoid loud noises and vibrations.** The tank should not be near a washing machine, nor should it be near loud loudspeakers.

3. **Avoid cold drafts and heaters.** Do not open the window on a cold winter day if you have the aquarium right underneath. Do not place it too close to the radiator either, leave at least 50 centimeters of separation. This is important to keep the aquarium temperature stable. If your aquarium is larger than 60-100 liters the temperature changes are more progressive, but if your passion are small aquariums of 20 liters, you can have major problems with temperature changes.

4. Maintain an environment free of insecticides, cleaning products or other potentially toxic products around the aquarium.

5. Make sure there is at least one **outlet nearby.**

6. **Do not place electrical appliances under the aquarium**. However, the filter and other accessories can be placed there.

7. If you have **dogs or cats,** we recommend **that** there are no nearby surfaces from which to reach the tank. In your particular case, you may need to cover the tank, especially if you have cats.

8. Consider how much space the filter will take up (if it is a backpack filter) and how much space you will run the tubing through (if it is an external filter). If you stick it too close to a wall, there may not be enough room.

9. Provide **convenient access for maintenance**.

10. **Find a prominent place to enjoy the show it offers.**

If there are children at home, having the aquarium against a wall in the living room, for example, will reduce the probability of it being hit by accident. And, if it is also in a corner, in the event of being hit, the table will have two supports: one at the back and one on the side.

AQUARIUM FILTRATION. FILTER AND FILTER MEDIA.

Introduction to chapters 3, 4 and 5. Filtration is probably the most important part of the project; an essential element to achieve and maintain water quality. **The main function** is to **transform the toxic substances** resulting from the decomposition of organic matter **into less toxic ones.** The filtration equipment is mainly composed of: **filter + filtering material**.

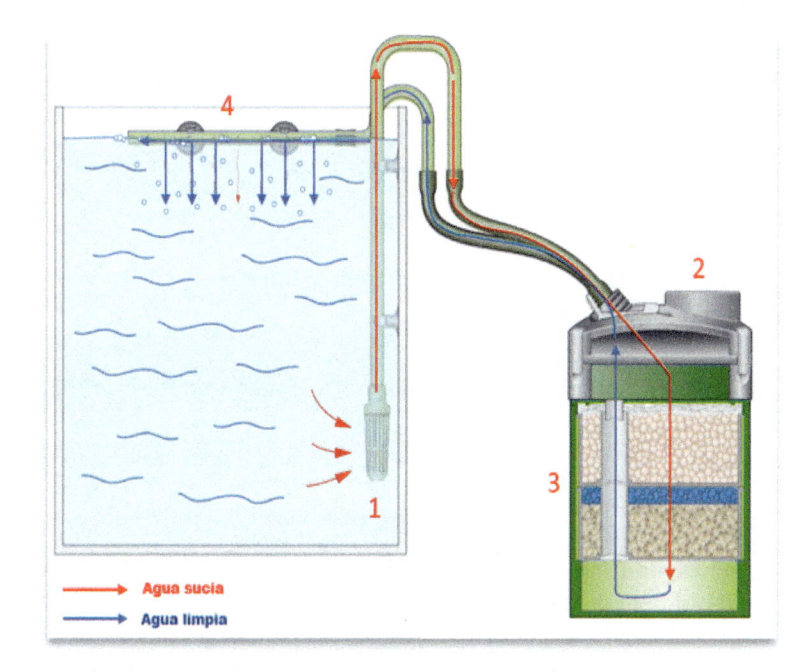

These toxic substances are: **ammonia or ammonium (NH4+) and nitrites (NO2-). All three are very toxic** to fish and other animals. **The filtration equipment will transform them into nitrates (NO3-). This transformation is carried out by the nitrifying bacteria** that live in the biological filter material inside the filter. We will develop a brief introduction below and repeat these concepts later.

In aquariums with abundant **natural plants**, they play an **important role in the filtration and detoxification** of the water. They are capable of removing large amounts of nitrates and ammonia. They can also remove heavy metals and provide the ecosystem with other benefits that will be discussed in the section on plants in chapter 12.

In the picture we see a filter that pumps "dirty water" into its interior, so that it passes through the filtering material. This will transform the toxic substances. Finally, "clean water" is refilled to the tank.

This chapter, the plants chapter (12) and chapter 9: "The importance of water" are the ones that most influence **water quality** and are, therefore, the most important to avoid diseases in our animals, algae and the rest of the problems we can have in our aquariums.

Here is a brief introduction, it is important to understand these concepts:

Water filtration consists mainly in the transformation of toxic substances (ammonium and nitrites) into much less toxic ones (nitrates). Secondly, it can also remove particles that remain floating in the water column. And, thirdly, it can have other more specific functions that we will see later. **Filtration occurs mainly in the filtration equipment and plant metabolism** (in aquariums with natural plants).

Toxic substances: **ammonium and ammonia, nitrites** and to a lesser extent nitrates. Toxic substances arise from fish wastes and from the decomposition of organic matter in the aquarium: food, dead animals or plants, etc. If these toxic

33

substances accumulate in the aquarium, they will cause our fish to become sick and die, trigger algae growth, cloudy water, etc.

The filtration equipment. The filtration equipment is composed of:

- **A filter.** A pump, which will take the water from the tank, pass it through the filter material and refill it back to the tank.

- **Filter material. The key component in filtration**. It is located inside the filter, arranged in layers (usually). It can be of **3 types** in the freshwater aquarium: mechanical filtration, biological filtration and chemical filtration.

    Of the three types, there is only one that is really essential in "almost" any ecosystem: "biological filter media". Biological filter media contains nitrifying bacteria, which are responsible for transforming ammonium and nitrites into nitrates.

Natural plants. In planted aquariums, plants play an essential role in the ecosystem. They acquire functions such as the following:

- Water **filtration and detoxification**. They are capable of removing large amounts of nitrates and ammonia.
- **Remove heavy metals** that may be toxic to fish or other animals.
- **Algae growth control.**
- **They oxygenate the water and reduce CO2.** Although air probably provides more oxygen to the water than plants.
- **They prevent the substrate from becoming toxic.** Plants keep the substrate healthy and it will rarely need to be vacuumed.

All these benefits can replace some of the aquarist's labor: reducing water changes, cleaning and vacuuming of gravel or sand and improving filtration, even allowing to reduce filtration equipment.

And that is all. These are the most important concepts about filtration and they are the ones you need to know.

There are also nitrifying bacteria in the substrate and in the water column, but in smaller quantities. For proper aquarium filtration you will have to choose a filter and filter media that fits the size of your tank, the amount and type of fish you will have, the presence or not of natural plants and other characteristics of your project. We will see it later.

Remember: Get a good filter and good filter media! **Poor filtration equals poor water quality. And this is the origin of the most frequent problems in our aquariums.**

There are colleagues who keep aquariums without filtration equipment and without specific filtering material. Of course, their aquariums also need biological filtration and their ecosystems contain nitrifying bacteria, although in smaller quantities. They achieve this by keeping decomposing organic matter in their aquariums to a minimum, **very few fish and animals**, little food and lots of plants that consume nitrates, nitrites and ammonium.

This is an example of an aquarium without filtration equipment: "**24th Month - (Carrot Feeding Frenzy) NO filter, NO CO2, NO Ferts 5 Gallon Nano Tank**" from the channel: Foo the Flowerhorn: https://www.youtube.com/watch?v=ptR7ngChDqs This book will help you to understand these ecosystems as well, we will give you the information that will allow you to develop all kinds of projects, so you can choose your personal one.

3 THE FILTER

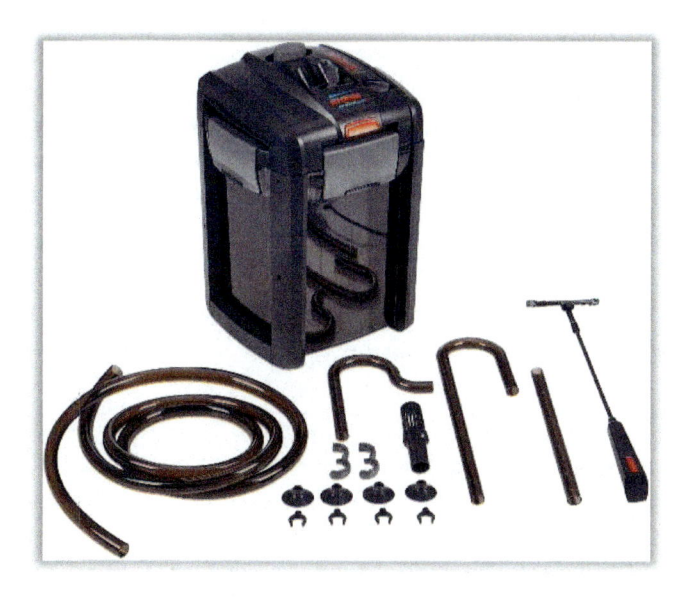

The most frequent mistake when we set up our first project is to buy an inadequate filter, or to buy an aquarium set with a bad filter. In an aquarium, the equipment components with the highest cost are, in general, the tank and the filter. In an aquarium with high plant requirements, it will be the lighting.

A good filter is a good investment: the secret to saving on the purchase of a filter is to make the right choice from the start.

Assuming that the filter is made with quality materials and with a good finish, the **2 most important characteristics of the filter are: the flow rate and the capacity for filtering material.**

3.1 THE TWO MOST IMPORTANT FEATURES OF THE FILTER

THE FLOW

The flow rate is measured in liters per hour that the filter is able to take from the tank, pass through it and refill to the tank. **The manufacturer always gives the data in "theoretical flow rate"**, which is the liters per hour that pass through the filter **WITHOUT filter material inside.** It is recommended that it be AT LEAST 3-5 times the total volume of your tank. **We recommend that it should be AT LEAST 5-6 times the total volume of the tank.** That is to say, if your tank is 100 liters, your filter should have a flow rate of at least 500 liters/hour. This will allow you to adapt it to almost any project for that tank.

The "actual flow rate". The real or effective flow is lower than the theoretical or marked by the manufacturer. When putting filtering materials, the water flow in the filter is reduced by about 30-40% (and can be reduced up to 50% from the beginning if we saturate all the filter capacity). When **buying the filter, we have to pay attention to the theoretical flow rate,** because it is the one given by the manufacturer, **and the type of filter** (as we will see later, an internal or backpack filter will saturate and reduce its flow rate before a canister type).

THE CAPACITY FOR FILTER MATERIAL

The filter media capacity is the space to hold filter media. Sometimes it is not easy to find this information, but it is important, especially in the "backpack" type filters and even more in the "internal" ones that are more limited in this aspect. **We recommend that it should be AT LEAST 1.5 liters per 100 liters of tank.** That is to say, if your tank is 100 liters, that your filter has a capacity of at least 1500 milliliters of filtering material. With this recommendation you will be able to adapt your filter for any type of project in the future. Although, like the flow rate, the actual capacity you need will depend on factors such as the filter material you are going to use and the characteristics of the project.

Example for a 200-liter aquarium. Filter characteristics:

For a 200-liter aquarium, you will need a filter with:

- A flow rate of at least 1200 liters per hour (**theoretical** flow rate, marked by the manufacturer).
- A filter media capacity of at least 3 liters.

There is NO problem if you "oversize" the filter (we buy one with a higher flow and capacity than we need). **Why?** Because all filters have a flow regulator. And there is no reason to occupy all the available capacity with filtering materials. We can always use the filter at 60% or 80% of its full functionality, **but if the filter you have bought is insufficient for your project working at 100% of its capacity, you will have to buy another one.**

In addition, as the weeks and months go by, the flow rate of the filter will decrease as the organic matter accumulates inside it. The greater the flow reserve and the more capacity you have without occupying the filter material, the longer you will be able to extend the cleaning periods.

Another objective we look for when buying a filter is that it should be efficient. An efficient filter. **It is a filter with a good balance between flow and capacity for filter material.** In the market you will find filters with very little capacity (less than 500ml) working with flow rates of more than 600l/h. This is especially frequent in internal filters. The water will often pass through very little filter material; filtration will be inefficient. **The external filters for aquarium "canister" type are the best option in this aspect.** The one in the image on the previous page is a good example of this type of filter. With large flow rates and large capacity for filtering material.

The intermediate option would be a backpack filter.

IS FLOW RATE OR CAPACITY MORE IMPORTANT?

BOTH! If we have a 100-liter aquarium and we are going to buy a filter with a higher flow rate than we need, but with a lower capacity, this filter is NOT suitable. And neither the other way around. Let's see it below:

For example: We are going to buy a backpack filter for **an "undemanding" 100-liter aquarium** (with few fish and little decomposing organic matter in general). Therefore, a flow rate of **at least 600 liters / hour** and a capacity of **at least 1.5 liters** will be sufficient. And we are in doubt whether to buy filter A or filter B.

Backpack filter A:

- Flow rate: 1000 liters/hour.
- Capacity: 1 liter.

THIS FILTER IS NOT SUITABLE: they have more flow than we need, there is no problem. But the capacity is less than we need. It is no good for us.

Clarification: *It may be useful for very specific projects such as an aquarium with few animals and with many natural plants that also favor water filtration.*

Backpack filter B:

- Flow rate: 1500 liters/hour.
- Capacity: 2 liters.

THIS FILTER IS THE RIGHT FILTER: they have more flow than we need, no problem. They have more capacity than we need, no problem.

In another hypothetical case, in which the flow rate is the criterion that is not met, it would not be a suitable filter either. The filter has to meet both criteria.

What we have just seen are the basics for choosing a filter. We will develop it a little further, so that the filter is best suited to your specific project.

3.2 HOW DOES A FILTER WORK?

The mechanism is simple, and is similar in all types of filters. **A filter consists of**:

- A water inlet pipe
- A water suction pump
- A compartment containing the filter media
- One water outlet

The simplest models have a single compartment to place the filtering material. The rest are divided into several compartments or "baskets".

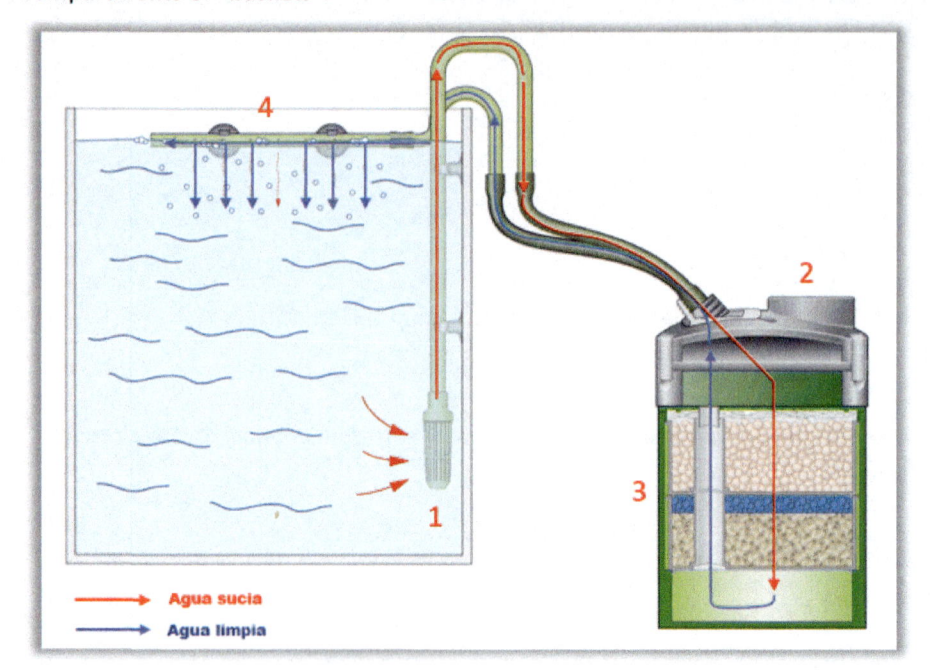

The diagram in the image represents a canister external filter. The arrows indicate the water flow. The "dirty water" arrives at the filter. It passes through the compartments where the filter material is. And finally, the "clean water" is refilled to the aquarium. **In this example the filter media are not well placed**, let's see how to do it!

→ Agua sucia
→ Agua limpia

DIRECTION OF WATER FLOW AND PLACEMENT OF FILTER MEDIA

1. **Water inlet** from the tank. The water contains solid particles (such as food debris, animal waste, plant leaves, etc.) as well as toxic substances (ammonium, ammonia and nitrites, etc.).
2. **Filter head,** where the water pump is located, which allows the water to advance through the pipe system and inside the filter.
3. **Compartments or baskets,** in which the filtering materials are located.

    The water must pass through the different compartments in the following order:

    - **1st mechanical filter** (if any): which retains the largest particles.
    - **2nd the biological filter (ALWAYS PRESENT)**: home to nitrifying bacteria that transform ammonia and nitrites into nitrates.
    - **3º Finally, chemical filter** (if any): we will see its functions later on.

4. **Clean water outlet** that is refilled to the tank.

Later on, we will talk about 2 filters that we recommend for their good results and **you will see how to put the filtering material.**

3.3 TYPES OF FILTERS

The market is large and the options are diverse. There are a **multitude of filters**, both for the smallest aquariums or nano aquariums and for aquariums with volumes greater than 600 liters.

Each system has its advantages and disadvantages, but **you will always have several optimal options for your project.**

A. INTERNAL FILTERS

Internal filters are those that are placed inside the tank. In general, we do not recommend their use. They can be useful for aquariums of less than 40-60 liters, but even in these cases we recommend the use of backpack filters. This is not to say that there are no good options on the market; there are colleagues who are using them with good results.

They are placed inside the tank. They stand out for their compact size and for being submerged, their operation is generally silent. Although there are internal filters that make noise and external filters that do not. Normally, they have an unbalanced flow/capacity ratio. Much flow and little capacity for filtering material. They are also often single compartment filters.

Some of the advantages of these filters are:

- They do not take up space outside the aquarium.
- You will not have problems with water leaks.
- We do not need to set up a cabinet to contain the filter (although not in the case of backpack filters either).

Some disadvantages:

- They take up space in the aquarium and can be an aesthetic problem.
- They usually have a smaller capacity for filter media. And **the larger the capacity for filter media, the more space they take up in the aquarium.**
- **In the maintenance we will dirty the** aquarium **water by** releasing part of its content.

B. CASCADE OR BACKPACK FILTERS.

They are not synonyms, but we will use them as such. Cascade filters are knapsack filters, but not all knapsack filters are cascade filters (you can see the difference in the pictures).

These are external filters that hang on the outside of one of the aquarium walls, with the water absorption hose and the waterfall or outlet tube inside the aquarium.

As the filter is outside the aquarium, they allow manufacturers to increase the size of the compartments, without reducing the volume of the interior of the tank. They are usually divided into compartments. Generally, they have a larger capacity for filter media than internal filters, but less than external filters.

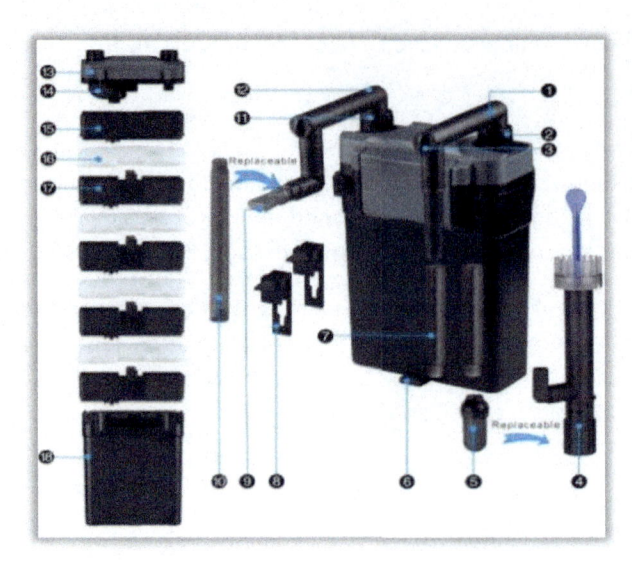

Some advantages of backpack filters:

- They do not take up space inside the ballot box.
- In general, since they are not limited by the space inside the tank, they have a greater capacity for filter media than internal filters.
- They are easy to handle. This will facilitate maintenance or other purposes.
- They are more economical than external filters.

Some disadvantages:

- They will be seen hanging out of the aquarium unless you put them in the back and cover the back glass with a backing paper. Another option is to put tall plants.
- In cascade filters it is not possible to prevent the water from falling on the surface, which facilitates the input of O_2 into the water and the output of CO_2. This can be a drawback for hobbyists with planted aquariums with high requirements using artificial CO_2.
- With respect to external canister filters, there is a greater limitation in size and they have a smaller capacity for the filter material.

C. EXTERNAL OR "CANISTER" TYPE FILTERS

These filters are placed separately from the tank. They are connected to it by an inlet and an outlet hose.

In general, they are filters with a high flow rate and large capacity for filter material. They can be perfectly used from 50-70 liters tanks. Aesthetically they also have advantages: the filter can be stored in the cabinet containing the tank, leaving only the tubes in view.

In this type of filter, it must be taken into account that **a larger inlet and outlet pipe allows a higher flow rate to pass through.**

Some advantages of external filters:

- They do not have a capacity or flow limitation.
- Because they are out of sight you can buy large filters, suitable for your needs whatever they may be.
- They do not take up space inside or hanging in the tank.

- They are easy to handle for maintenance: adjustments, change of filtering material, cleaning...
- There are very quiet models (of any of the three types).
- Long periods without maintenance. Due to their high capacity, they can go for months without saturation and without decreasing their flow rate.
- Many models have pre-filters that can further extend the maintenance period.

Some disadvantages:

- It would be advisable to install a cabinet with a cabinet under the aquarium to place the filter there, for aesthetic reasons.
- The prices are, in general, higher than those of backpack filters. Although the reality is that, when comparing an external filter and a backpack filter of the same range and price, the capacity for filtering material is equal or higher in external filters.
- There is a higher risk of water leakage than in the previous types due to poor maintenance.

3.4 OTHER ASPECTS OF CHOOSING THE FILTER FOR YOUR PROJECT

- Volume of the tank
- Number of fish, species and their diet
- Planted or unplanted aquarium
- Filter materials
- Maintenance

Tank volume. As we told you in the introduction of the chapter, the total volume of water in your aquarium should pass at least 3-5 times through the filter in one hour. For this, the filter should have a theoretical flow rate of at least 5-6 times the volume of the aquarium. The capacity for filter material that we generally recommend is **at least** 1.5 liters per 100 liters of water. **The larger the volume of the tank, the higher the flow rate and capacity of the filter should be**.

Number of fish, species and their feeding. Another important factor when choosing a filter, is to take into account, approximately, which are the species of fish that will inhabit the aquarium and their type of feeding. There are fish that produce more waste than others and there are types of feeding that "pollute" more than others. For example, if you have or want to have an aquarium with "discus fish", and you are going to feed them with food, you will have to take into account that these generate a lot of decomposing organic matter. Your filter will need enough filter media and water flow to transform these toxics.

The same applies to "Goldfish", which also produce a lot of waste. In addition, "swim bladder" problems are common in Goldfish and it is recommended not to feed dry food. By soaking flakes or other food before putting them in the aquarium, more waste will be generated and more organic matter will accumulate in the water.

The number of fish in the aquarium is even more important than the species.

In short, **if we have overpopulation in the aquariums, if we feed with slurry, if we have fish that produce a lot of waste...** All these situations should be taken into account before buying the filter to **increase the recommended capacity for filter material, for example, up to 2 or 3 liters of capacity per 100 liters of tank.** As for the flow rate, 600-700 liters per hour per 100 liters would continue to be sufficient in canister filters and probably have to be higher for backpack or internal filters, since their actual flow rate will decrease by a greater percentage with the addition of the filter media and with the accumulation of waste products.

Don't forget that no matter how much filter media and bacteria you have in the filter, nitrates will continue to build up. If you have a lot of decomposing matter in the aquarium, you will have to increase the frequency or the percentage of water you replace at each water change **or put in natural plants**. Another option would be to use special chemical filtration (this is explained in chapter 4: "filter media" and at the end of the book, in "Appendix 1".

Planted or unplanted aquariums. In aquariums with abundant **natural plants**, they play an **important role in the filtration and detoxification** of the water. They are capable of removing large amounts of nitrates, ammonia and phosphates. They can also remove heavy metals and provide the ecosystem with other benefits that will be discussed in the section on plants in chapter 12.

On the other hand, **if you have a "high-tech aquarium"** (later, in the plants section of chapter 12, we will see better what this concept means, however, we leave here below a video of a colleague where he explains it), with plants that grow quickly, with frequent pruning and frequent leaf replacement, it is possible that your filter is saturated with large debris of decaying leaves. **You may need a filter with a higher capacity and flow rate to avoid frequent saturation** and prolong maintenance periods.

- **In an aquarium with high plant requirements**, with fertilizer and CO2, we recommend:
    - **500ml or less of biological filter media per 100 liters** of tank or follow the manufacturer's minimum recommendations.
    - **3 liters of total capacity per 100 liters** of tank.
    - A **theoretical flow rate** of at least **7-9 times** the total aquarium volume.
    - The **use of mechanical filtration** could be very useful in this case.

"An example of high-tech aquarium"

- **In an aquarium with <u>many</u> plants of low to medium requirements, healthy, with a low to medium amount of lighting, no fertilizer and no CO2 and no overpopulation of fish or other animals:**
  - **You can also use 500ml or less of biological filter media per 100 liters** (or follow the manufacturer's minimum recommendations).
  - **Follow general recommendations** (at least 1500 ml total capacity and 500 l/h flow rate).

"An example of medium-tech aquarium"

- In aquariums with few plants, we can act as if there were no plants and continue with the following recommendations.

Filter media. The most important filtering material and **the ONLY ONE THAT IS ESSENTIAL IS: the biological filtering material.** But there are projects or very specific situations that may require the use of other filtering materials, and in that case, **you can NOT remove the biological filtration to put other types of filtration. You will need to have that space previously, even if most of the time you have it in disuse**.

Maintenance. The smaller the capacity and the lower the flow rate of our filter, the more attentive we will have to be with the weekly care of our aquarium to avoid the accumulation of decomposing organic matter and the saturation of the filtration equipment. We will see how to do a good maintenance in chapter 10. In **addition, if we have a filter with a very tight maximum flow and very saturated with filtering material, its water flow will decrease more easily and we will have to clean the filter before.**

3.5 WHAT CAPACITY AND FLOW RATE SHOULD YOUR FILTER HAVE IN YOUR PARTICULAR CASE?

GENERAL RECOMMENDATIONS

1. **Filter capacity per 100 liters of water**.
   - At least 500 ml of biological filter material.
   - At least 1500 ml total capacity.

   This capability will have to be looked for in the description of each filter (not always easy to find).

2. **Theoretical flow rate of the filter per 100 liters of water**.
   - At least 500-600 liters per hour.

SPECIAL RECOMMENDATIONS

- In case of discus aquariums, goldfish or other fish that generate a **lot of organic waste**.
- In case you are going to include **more fish than recommended** (in general 1 cm of fish per liter of water, we will see it in chapter 14: "The inhabitants of the aquarium").
- In case you want to spend as **little time as** possible on **maintenance** tasks.

For these cases we recommend:

- **Filter capacity per 100 liters of water**.
    - At least 1000-1500 ml of biological filter material.
    - At least 2500 ml total capacity.

- **Theoretical filter flow per 100 liters of water**.
    - At least 700-800 liters per hour.

<u>**In case of heavily planted aquariums**</u>, whether they are being fertilized or not, and whether you are using artificial CO_2 or not, the biological **filter media requirements are likely to be lower than the general recommendations**. Two pages back we have seen specific recommendations for this particular case.

OUR PERSONAL RECOMMENDATION: OVERSIZE THE FILTRATION EQUIPMENT

Why? It is possible that for your current project you do not need a more powerful filter, but **there is no problem if you have extra capacity**, this will **allow you to relax with the maintenance** of your current project. Besides, in the future, **it will be useful for any project** you want to set up in that tank.

The investment of oversizing the filter now is minor compared to the cost of having to buy a new one in the future. And finally, keep in mind that a good filter will last you many years and some brands have spare parts for each of the components.

- **Filter capacity per 100 liters of water**.
    - **At least 1000-1500 ml of biological filter material** (except in aquariums with many natural plants).
    - **At least 3000 ml total capacity.**
- **Theoretical flow rate of the filter per 100 liters of water.**
    - **At least 800-1000 liters per hour.**

3.6 TWO EXAMPLES OF RECOMMENDED FILTERS

Of course, there are many more filters with good value for money that may be suitable for your aquarium and of many recognized brands such as "JBL", "Tetra", "Fluval", "Sera"... We will name two, with which we have had good experience, as an example.

We will see them in the following pages...

EXTERNAL FILTER: EHEIM PRO

This is one of the best external filters on the market in recent years. The filter includes ALL the filter media you need.

There are 3 models of different sizes and flow rates. **The smallest is the "250", with a pump flow rate of 950 l / h and a volume for filter material of 3.5 liters.** You will find the other two models easily on Google in your aquarium store.

These are some of the features to look for first when looking for a filter:

- A reliable brand that ensures a good finish?
- Does it include filter media?
- Is the flow rate and capacity listed in the product description?
- In external filters, what is the maximum height to which the water can be pumped?
- What is the power consumption and is there much difference with others of similar characteristics?
- What are the dimensions of the filter?
- What are the diameters of the inlet and outlet pipes?

According to our personal recommendation to oversize the filter, it would be **an ideal filter for an aquarium of 80-100 liters.** But depending on what projects, it can be used for aquariums up to 200 liters. **The 250 model**, you will **find it from 190 euros.**

Next, we will look at one of the most economical filters on the market...

Nicepets - External Filter.

We go to the other extreme, one of the most economical external filters on the market. There are 2: one with a flow rate up to 1000 liters/hour and another one up to 1200 liters/hour. We do not know the capacity for filtering material that they have inside, but for its size, in the case of the 1000 l/h model it should be around 3.5-4 liters. These filters do not include the filtering material you need.

Price: 70 euros. (90 euros with the filtering material)

You can also find high-flow external filters with a large capacity for filter media on AliExpress, such as those from the Sunsun brand. The main issue with these filters is the lack of references and experience with them. However, in the case of Sunsun, this brand has already developed several filters with a quality-to-price ratio that's hard to beat in the market, among other aquarium products. It's not easy to find reviews from people who have actually used these filters. They are available on Amazon and AliExpress, and perhaps soon they may start to become available in some specialized aquarium stores.

If we look at the prices, we will see that **the difference between an Eheim brand filter,** of the characteristics we have mentioned**, compared to Sunsun or Nicepets** (after including the price of the filter material) **would be around 60 euros**. It is possible that this type of cheaper filters has a good quality-price ratio, that spare parts start to exist and that they are a good purchase option, but we cannot assure you that. You will have to decide for yourself whether to venture out in search of the best value for money or spend a little more in exchange for greater safety. In the case of taking the risk, a Sunsun brand filter might be our recommendation at this time.

Later we will see how to assemble them.

BACKPACK FILTER: SEACHEM TIDAL

When it comes to hang-on-back filters, we'd like to introduce you to one from a well-known brand, Seachem. However, there are many other brands that offer good products as well. These filters are generally more affordable than external filters, and the price difference (for filters with similar features) between one from a reputable brand like Seachem and one from an unknown brand is typically between 10 and 30 euros when considering the price of filter materials.

Seachem Tidal Backpack Filter

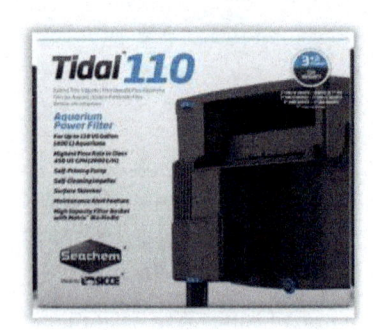

There are several models with lower or higher capacity for filter media and lower or higher flow rates. **All of them include a good filtering material.** We recommend its use from 20-30 liters aquariums.

Tidal 35:	Tidal 55:
Flow rate of 500L/h.	Flow rate of 1000L/h.
Capacity of 0.7 liters.	Capacity of 1.2 liters.
From 50 euros.	From 45 euros.
Tidal 75:	**Tidal 110:**
Flow rate of 1500L/h.	Flow rate of 2000L/h.
Capacity of 1.9 liters.	Capacity of 3.2 liters.
From 75 euros.	From 95 euros.

In the table on the previous page, we leave you the 4 models that are on the market. According to the "general recommendation" for the choice of the filter, the Tidal 75 filter for a tank of about 100 liters would be a suitable filter. Although depending on the project, it might be necessary to oversize the filter. Probably, **using the Tidal 110 for 100-liter tank, you will be able to develop almost any project in that tank.**

Of course, you can find other quality backpack filters on the market from other brands.

In the case of backpack filters, we recommend that you get one of a known brand. For similar filtering material capacity and flow rates, we see that **the price difference**, when we take into account the **purchase of filtering materials, IS BETWEEN 0 AND 20 EUROS!** for a filter that you will have for years. As for the **store where to buy the filters, very simple, remember:** put the name of the filter in Google followed by the word buy and get the best deal! And keep in mind that a good option will also be to get it in a reliable aquarium store.

WHAT ABOUT INTERNAL FILTERS?

In Best Aquarium we do NOT usually recommend them because of the lower capacity for filter media. To have a sufficient capacity for filter media would have to subtract much volume to the interior of the tank.

Although we usually do not recommend them, it is true that there may be suitable models for your aquarium. If in your particular case you need one of these filters, take **into account the same recommendations of flow rate and filter material capacity as for the other types of filters**.

There are other filtration systems such as **plate or bottom filters**. These are placed under the gravel, and collect the dirty water that enters the filter from under the gravel, which helps to keep it always clean. They also have other disadvantages such as the difficulty to maintain natural plants in good conditions in these aquariums.

A big step!

Following the recommendations in the previous chapter for the choice of the filter is a great step to start developing your project. Let's now look at the filter media, the key to good filtration.

4 THE FILTER MATERIAL

As important as the choice of filter is the choice of filter material. We are interested in 3 types: mechanical, biological and chemical.

There is something that greatly simplifies this issue, and that is that **there is only one type of filtration that is essential in our aquariums: <u>biological filtration.</u>** As we have said before, it is in charge of carrying out the most important part of the filtration of an aquarium: the transformation of toxic substances into less toxic ones.

On the other hand, <u>mechanical filtration</u> will help us to remove particles in suspension, being dispensable its use. That is to say, we can have an aquarium with water with visible size particles in suspension and still have a healthy and balanced ecosystem. It would be like when the sea water is "churned up", with remains of algae and other particles in suspension and there is no imbalance in the ecosystem.

Finally, <u>chemical filtration</u> can be used at specific times to remove certain compounds from the water.

4.1 MECHANICAL FILTRATION

Generally, some type of synthetic material such as polyester (perlon) or foam sponge is used. Brands such as Sera have developed products that can be very useful as the "Sera cristal clear", balls with a filtering capacity similar to perlon, but without the saturation problems that this one has. In addition, they can be cleaned and are reusable. You can find more information on Google or in your trusted aquarium store.

If present, this is the first layer through which the water has to pass when it reaches the filter. There are other options in terms of materials, such as "plastic balls", but they are not particularly interesting, take up a lot of space and **the function is always the same: to retain suspended particles in the aquarium water** (pieces of leaves, food debris, fish waste, small particles detached from the aquarium substrate, etc.).

51

What happens if I don't use mechanical filter media? Generally, **nothing** relevant. **The water quality will remain optimal.** It is possible, however, that small particles may begin to appear in suspension in the water column and may pose an aesthetic problem, but it is also possible that this does not occur. Another problem that could occur is that our biological and/or chemical material becomes saturated with particles and loses part of its function so we would have to maintain the filtration equipment more frequently.

TO USE OR NOT TO USE MECHANICAL FILTER MEDIA?

If you do NOT have enough capacity in your filter to put the minimum amount of biological material that we have **recommended** in the previous chapter (at least 500ml per 100 liters): **DO NOT put mechanical filtration and use a good quality biological material.**

One option in this case is to install a **"pre-filter"**: a Foam sponge, usually in the form of a hollow cylinder, which is placed in the filter inlet pipe.

It will not allow the passage of larger suspended particles into the filter and will lengthen the filter maintenance periods. In refill you will have to remove and clean the sponge approximately every 3-5 days, depending on its size. The cleaning of this prefilter can be done with tap water.

It will also be advisable to use a prefilter in aquariums with a large amount of organic matter, such as high-tech planted aquariums, in order not to saturate the filter and extend the maintenance periods. It can also be useful if you are breeding shrimp or fry in your aquarium, as it will prevent them from being absorbed by the filter.

Remember to remove the pre-filter if you go on vacation, if it becomes saturated, it will considerably decrease the flow rate of the filter and will not fulfill its functions.

If you have already put at least the minimum amount of biological material that we have recommended in the previous chapter, **you can put some mechanical filtration. In** any case, **we recommend the use of foam sponge, but NOT the use of perlon.** Perlon significantly shortens filter maintenance periods, as it quickly saturates and clogs the water passage.

In chapter 5 "How to set up the filter" we will see an example with the Eheim Pro 4 external filter: **A 1.5-2 cm layer of foam sponge may be enough mechanical filter material for a filter with a filter material capacity of 3 liters.** If we would like to add some more mechanical filtration we could use Sera balls, for example. Use this as a reference.

Also, there are cylindrical filters with a metal grid, these do not become saturated and require much less frequent maintenance. They are even better than sponge filters if your goal is to prevent small animals from entering the filter.

WHAT MECHANICAL FILTER MEDIA DO YOU NEED AND WHERE TO BUY IT?

If you use only one, we recommend the foam sponge. A coarse or medium pore sponge and **avoid, in general, the use of perlon wool**. A possible use of perlon would be: if you have just removed the substrate, for example, and you have lifted a lot of particles, you can use it temporarily. (You can also wait 24 or 48 hours until it settles again without any problem).

- **External canister filter:** you can put the sponge inside the filter. You can also use a pre-filter.
- **Backpack filter:** having the most limited space, it prioritizes the biological filtering material and the water flow. If you have followed our recommendations, you can also put some mechanical filtration inside.

If for reasons of your personal project, you decide to put more than one layer of mechanical filtration, the mechanical filter should go from coarser to finer pore.

Many filters already include the sponge for mechanical filtration with the purchase. **Check if the sponge is included or not in your filter before buying it.** Perlon wool is also often included, our recommendation is to remove all of it, especially if you have little capacity for biological filtration.

Remember: The prefilter is the only filter media in your filter that you can clean with tap water. The rest of the filter media will need to be cleaned with aquarium water or according to the manufacturer's instructions in the case of some types of chemical filtration.

The mechanical filtration inside the filter can be cleaned with both aquarium water and tap water. The filter and its components can also be cleaned with tap water. If you do NOT do it according to these instructions, part or all of the bacteria living in the biological filter material will die and cease to perform their functions.

To purchase prefilter sponge or metal grid

- The cheapest: go to AliExpress and type in the search engine: "aquarium prefilter sponge or metal grid". You will have for several years.
- The quickest, and for some folks the ideal, is to go to a reputable aquarium store and buy your equipment there. It may be a little less economical than looking for the best deals on Google, but there are professionals who can help you if you have any doubts.
- Another option is to enter Amazon and write in the search engine: "aquarium prefilter".

To purchase the filter sponge:

- The cheapest: go to AliExpress and type in the search engine: "aquarium filter sponge". For 4 euros you will have sponge for life.
- The quickest, and for some folks the ideal, is to go to a reputable aquarium store and buy your equipment there. It may be a little less economical than looking for the best deals on Google, but there are professionals who can help you if you have any doubts.
- Another option is to go to Amazon and type in the search engine: "aquarium filter sponge". Choose a medium-large pore. For 5-10 euros you will have a sponge for life.

4.2 BIOLOGICAL FILTRATION

Following the water circulation direction: the biological filtering material is placed after the foam sponge (if any) or first (if there is no sponge). It performs the most important function: **it houses the nitrifying bacteria,** capable of transforming ammonium, ammonia and nitrites (product of fish waste and decomposition of organic matter in the aquarium) into a less toxic compound, nitrates. **Nitrifying bacteria are aerobic: they need oxygen to live. This process is known as nitrification.**

The biological filter media layer consists of ceramic or other equally porous materials. The more porous the material, the more space for bacteria to settle and proliferate.

There are some biological materials such as De Nitrate and Matrix from Seachem, which, because they have such high porosity, can have anaerobic conditions (or lack of oxygen) and **also remove nitrates** from the water. That is, **there are also bacteria that can remove nitrates. These are anaerobic bacteria. This process is known as denitrification** and would eliminate the most frequent toxicant in our aquariums completely, expelling it out of the water in the form of N_2 which is the gas that makes up 78% of the air in our atmosphere. **This aspect is NOT as relevant as it may seem**, since it is a slow process, which needs specific conditions to occur in our aquariums, and that will not occur to a sufficient extent in our aquariums to prevent us from having to do water changes. Denitrification also occurs under the substrate and in poorly oxygenated areas of our aquarium or filter (with poor water circulation).

In addition to discussing chemical filtration, we will also discuss other methods of lowering nitrate levels in our aquariums in "Appendix 1".

As soon as the aquarium and filter are set up, the biological filter material will be completely empty, without bacterial colonies, so your aquarium will have to go through a process known as cycling, during which the nitrifying bacteria settle: we will see this in chapter 9.

There are some biological filter media that can modify water parameters such as pH. We recommend that, if you are NOT setting up a very specific project and if you do not know exactly what you are looking for, use inert or neutral materials (that do not modify the water parameters).

We have insisted a lot on the importance of the quality of the material, **NOT just any biological filtering material is useful. Look for a recognized brand and make a good investment in filtration.** These materials have a life of **at least two years**, so their cost is not really as high as it may seem. If it is a good material, it will be enough to make a 10% change of the material every one-two year by replacing it with a new one. Many filters already include the biological filtration material with the purchase. **Check whether or not it is included with your filter before you buy it.**

WHAT BIOLOGICAL FILTER MEDIA DO YOU NEED AND WHERE TO BUY IT?

We propose 3 options that give good results. Any of the three is a good option, although of course there are many other good quality options for sale:

- Neo Media Pure 1 liter for approx. 14 euros.
- Seachem Matrix 500mL for approx. 14 euros.
- JBL Micromec 1 liter for approx. 13 euros.

As for the question of where to buy it, in this case it is very simple, you can search them on Google by putting the name of the product or go to your trusted store and choose one there.

There is a biological filtration system known as "trickling filter system" or "wet-dry filter" for which "bioballs" are used, although nowadays any type of biological material is also used. To use this system requires other types of filters and more space. They are an option to consider for very dedicated aquarists, with large aquariums or with several aquariums connected to a single filtration system. This type of filtration is not necessary for a good functioning of our ecosystems.

4.3 CHEMICAL FILTRATION

Chemical filtration can remove specific compounds from the water, such as organic matter, drugs, ammonium, nitrites, nitrates, phosphates, silica, etc. And it can also modify water parameters: GH, pH... There is a wide variety of chemical filtration products, each with its own functions and properties. They are used to optimize water conditions in very specific cases. The use of chemical filtration in an aquarium must have a specific objective:

SOME OF THE POSSIBLE USES OF CHEMICAL FILTRATION ARE AS FOLLOWS

- Remove organic matter degradation products (proteins, fats, fats, metals, hormones...) and also nitrate, nitrites, ammonium, phosphates... from the water in NON-PLANTED aquariums **to reduce the number of water changes and limit the appearance of algae.** They can also remove other compounds.
- Remove degradation products of organic matter (proteins, fats, fats, metals, hormones...) and also nitrate, nitrites, ammonium, phosphates... with activated carbon or another product, both in planted and unplanted aquariums to **solve a problem (temporarily) of excess ammonium.**
- Change the pH or hardness of the water.
- Eliminate medications after treatment.
- Eliminate unpleasant odors.
- Eliminate tannins released by wood if we have put in a new trunk. The water will be yellow.
- And many more.

The chemical load would be placed last in the water flow direction inside our filter, after the biological filtration. Even an additional filter could be used to place chemical filtration on an ad hoc basis.

Keep in mind that: if you have plants in the aquarium and you always leave a chemical load in the filter that eliminates the micronutrients and macronutrients they need to grow, there will be no nutrients for the plants, they will not grow and if this situation is maintained over time, they will eventually die.

The chemical filtering material par excellence has always been <u>activated carbon</u>, easy to obtain, affordable and very functional. But other options have been developed, such as adsorbent resins, which have some advantages over activated carbon. Resins can be used for specific purposes such as adsorbing and reducing the concentration of phosphates in the water (as a prevention against algae), absorbing* calcium and magnesium ions to reduce water hardness, or absorbing nitrates and nitrites. There are also acidifying peats, which add tannic and humic acids to the water, which lower the pH of the aquarium.

*Adsorber: this is the first time we refer to this concept. **Adsorption** is a process by which atoms, ions or molecules of dissolved gases, liquids or solids are retained on a surface, as opposed to **absorption**, which is a volume phenomenon.

If you are interested in this topic and want to expand a little more information, we will leave it for the end, as it is slightly more complex to understand and is not essential. You will find it in "Annex 1" at the end of the book.

WHAT CHEMICAL FILTER MEDIA DO YOU NEED AND WHERE TO BUY IT?

<u>NONE</u>. Save the 20, 40 or even 60 euros that you can spend on these materials. **The chemical filtering material that is capable of removing the greatest variety of different compounds from the water is activated carbon, so having it available at home is a good option to temporarily solve a problem.** If you are interested in these materials for a specific purpose or you have a problem that you need to solve temporarily, we will see how to do it at the end.

Remember that you will not only have to buy the filter material but also have space in the filter to use it. If you have an emergency and need chemical filtration to remove a compound from the water, we recommend the use of activated carbon, but remember to inform yourself well beforehand about its use.

WHY NOT USE CHEMICAL FILTER MEDIA WIDELY?

- They have a relatively high cost (around 15-20 euros each product and depending on the size of your tank).
- They require extra capacity in the filter or a second filter. Do not forget that the biological material is essential and it is possible that your filter does not have extra free space to put this material.
- It requires an extra time investment to learn how to use them and to replace them. Although their proper use can save you maintenance time and give you some interesting advantages in the medium to long term.
- In general, we will not be able to have natural plants if we use them.
- **And, above all, because its use is not necessary to maintain the balance in your ecosystem**: if you follow the advice we give you, you will have a healthy aquarium and you will avoid the most frequent diseases of your fish and the most frequent problems of your aquarium without the use of more products.

Remember: **NOT** to use chemical filtration media that removes organic matter, ammonium or nitrite **during the aquarium cycling process**; it will delay cycling.

4.4 FILTER MEDIA: KEY IDEAS

- **The choice of filter material and its quality is as important as the choice of filter.**
- Filtration occurs mainly (but not exclusively) inside the aquarium filter, thanks to filter media that are layered inside the filter.
- Aquarium water filtration can be of three types: mechanical, biological and chemical.
- The really essential one is biological filtration. And once this need is covered, secondly, you can also use mechanical filtration.

- Chemical filtration can be used at specific times to remove certain compounds or continuously for a specific purpose.

4.5 HOW TO PLACE THE FILTER MEDIA INSIDE THE FILTER?

We have already seen how to do it, but let's see it again a little more developed:

The position occupied by each type of filter material may vary from one filter to another, depending on the circuit followed by the water flow inside the filter:

- **From top to bottom:** the water enters the filter and passes through each compartment or basket in a downward direction until it reaches the base and ascends through one side until it exits the filter to be refilled to the tank. **In this case the 1st layer (the mechanical layer) would be at the top.**
- **From the bottom to the top:** The water arrives at the top of the filter and flows down through a pipe or side to the bottom and from there up through all the compartments of the filter to its outlet. **The 1st layer (the mechanical layer) would be at the bottom.**
- **Interspersed:** In one of the examples below (the Eheim pro 4 external filter) it happens that: the water arrives in the upper compartment of the filter, passes through a 1st layer of mechanical filtration and then falls to the base through a side tube. From the base, which would be the 2nd compartment, it rises to the central compartment, which would be the 3rd layer, and from there it is refilled to the aquarium again.

It is a simple thing, but it is not always equally evident in all filters. **You will have to spend 5 minutes to find out which is the circuit that follows the water in your filter**, it is important.

DIRECTION OF WATER FLOW

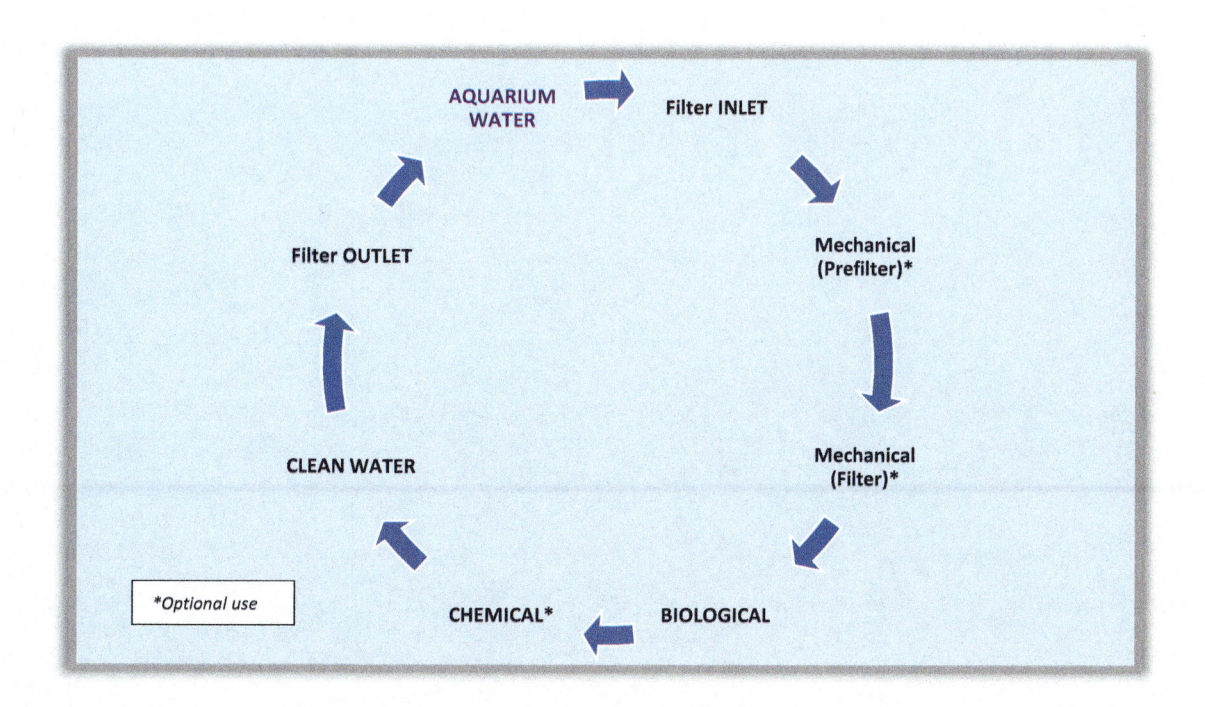

5 HOW TO SEP UP THE FILTER

We have seen how to choose the filtration equipment: a filter and the required filter media. Let's see 2 practical examples:

5.1 HOW TO SET UP AN EXTERNAL FILTER

Let's consider an example with the "EHEIM Professionel 4 external filter, model 350+":

As mentioned earlier, this filter comes with all the necessary filtering materials. It also includes some balls, plastic tubes, or spirals, which serve a mechanical filtration function and are optional. You can leave them unless you plan to use this compartment for other filtering materials, in which case, their removal is fine.

If, at some point, you require chemical filtration, you can remove these tubes or balls and use that basket for biological filtration, using the top basket for chemical filtration. Another option would be to remove the tubes and increase the amount of biological filtration using both compartments if needed for your particular project.

One aspect that may vary from one external filter to another is the water circuit within the filter. Spend a few minutes understanding the water flow inside your filter, as this will determine where you need to place the layers of filter material. Once you comprehend how this filter operates, you'll understand how others work as well.

The main difference between the 350+ model and the 250+ model is that the latter has one less basket. As shown, these filters already have the necessary filtering materials to start. At any time, part of this material can be replaced, especially the plastic baskets, with more useful materials.

We also mentioned the Nicepects filter, a lower-range external filter, for comparison with the Eheim. While **we don't have direct experience with this filter**, we present some aspects to consider when setting it up.

How to set up the Nicepets external filter?

It is assembled in a manner similar to the previous filter, always following the order: mechanical filtration first and then biological filtration. This filter does NOT include the necessary filter material. In the water flow diagram of the filter, **the water from the aquarium passes first through the lower basket:**

Steps to set up the filter:

1. Remove all the perlon that comes with the filter.
2. Purchase a foam sponge (mechanical material) and cut it to fit the shape of the basket. A medium thickness sponge of 2-3cm thickness will be enough.
3. Put it in the first basket through which the water from the aquarium passes.

4. You can also use a pre-filter in the water inlet pipe to the filter to prevent shrimp or small fish from being absorbed and to extend maintenance intervals.
5. Purchase the biological material of your choice (any of the three recommended brands is suitable). It's better to slightly exceed the required amount; if you use too little, ammonium and nitrites will accumulate in the water.
6. Fill the baskets with filter media to half their capacity or less. If you have an extra basket for other media (and you don't need to add anything at the moment), you can divide the biological media between the 2 baskets or leave it empty.
7. Fill the filter with aquarium water before closing it (without overflowing) and start it up!

5.2 HOW TO ASSEMBLE A BACKPACK FILTER

Let's consider an example with the "Seachem Tidal Backpack Filter":

Following the same order as the water flow direction: first, the mechanical filter material, and second, the biological filter material. You can obtain a medium-large porosity sponge, cut it to match the shape of the basket, and place it. A sponge thickness of 1.5-2cm will suffice in this example, and mechanical filtration is already included.

With this type of filter, if you don't reach the minimum recommended capacity, we recommend prioritizing biological filter media, at least 500mL per 100 liters. If you still have space, you can then add some mechanical filtration with a sponge. Whether you put a sponge inside the filter or not, you can use a pre-filter.

If you use NO mechanical filtration at all, not even a pre-filter, small visible particles **may** circulate in the water column. This is a matter of aesthetics, and your ecosystem will remain healthy and balanced. If you go on vacation, remember to remove the pre-filter.

In this case, the filter also includes ALL the necessary filtering material for use: Seachem's Matrix. No additional material would be necessary.

For those hobbyists who are starting out and have decided to do it in the simplest way and they have chosen a complete aquarium set, such as the "Marina complete aquarium set", we will explain how to set up the filter that is included, which is also applicable for similar cases:

Filtration for the "Marina complete aquarium set":

DO NOT follow the manufacturer's instructions and DO NOT use their replacement chemical filters that directly remove toxins from the water and must be changed every 4 weeks. It is true that, although you will not be able to have plants, if you follow the manufacturer's instructions, do a proper maintenance and do not put too many fish, your fish will live. But if you really want to create a healthy and stable ecosystem in your aquarium, with less maintenance and with the possibility of keeping plants, the steps are very similar to those to be followed with the rest of filters:

Empty ALL the baskets from the first day (If you already have fish in the aquarium when you change from chemical to biological material, the toxins will accumulate during the first month and your animals may die, so in this case you will have to phase out the chemical filtration).

1. Buy high-quality biological material and do not use mechanical filtration inside this filter (it does not have enough space).
2. Don't buy anything else! It is not necessary.
3. Fill the baskets with the biological material you have purchased.
4. The set includes a pre-filter sponge for the water inlet, use and clean it every 3-5 days.
5. If you go on vacation, simply remove the pre-filter.
6. That's it! Your filter is ready.

5.3 HOW TO SET UP AN INTERNAL FILTER

If you have read the two previous sections, there is not much more to add. Biological material is the priority, especially if it is a filter in which the capacity for the filter material is limited. Fill the filter with as much biological filter media as it will allow without completely saturating it so as not to reduce the water flow too much. In the event that you have more space after placing the biological filtering material (according to the quantities we recommend), you can add a first barrier of mechanical filtering material.

5.4 THE MOST IMPORTANT IDEA ABOUT THE FILTERING MATERIAL

The only essential filter material is biological. Manufacturers usually recommend 500ml of biological filter material per 200 liters. That might be too little for aquariums without natural plants, unless you have hardly any animals in them. If you don't have a filter yet or you are thinking of buying another one, **buy a filter with an oversized flow and capacity**, the price difference is not that high and **the best way to save is not having to buy the same thing twice.** *Use at least 500 ml of biological filtration per 100 liters.*

In specific cases, such as high-tech planted aquariums or low-tech aquariums with a large number of natural plants, you can reduce the amount of biological filter material.

Finally, in overcrowded aquariums, goldfish aquariums, discus aquariums or others where there is a very high amount of decomposing organic matter and without plants, *use at least 750-1000ml of biological filtration per 100 liters.*

Use high-quality biological filtration material.

6 AQUARIUM LIGHTING

Even if our aquarium only has fish and is not planted, lighting is still a must. **The fish and animals in our aquarium need to differentiate between day and night** and have stable routines. This means that you **will have to give them at least 7 - 9 hours of light per day**, if possible, always tanking it on and off at the same time. To do this, we recommend using a plug with a timer, as we will see in chapter 10.

If in your case you have **an aquarium without plants, the amount of light required is minimal**, and you will not need more than a system of fluorescent or LED tubes that fits your budget and the characteristics of the aquarium, and above all, your taste since you do not need anything more specific. You can also use RGB LED lights to highlight the colors of the fish.

On the other hand, if you would like to keep some plants, you will need a suitable lighting for your ecosystem and adapted to the characteristics of the plants you want to keep, with a minimum of power, intensity, and with specific characteristics.

Currently, there are many types of lighting available, the most commonly used being fluorescent tube and LED. T-5 or T-8 fluorescent tube lighting has been the most commonly used lighting in aquariums, but is being replaced by LEDs almost completely nowadays. As disadvantages with respect to the LED, they generate more heat, have a higher energy consumption and the average life of the tube is much lower than that of the LED.

6.1 GENERAL TIPS FOR LIGHTING YOUR AQUARIUM

- Due to their **durability, cost, power consumption** and proven excellent results in both planted and unplanted aquariums, **we recommend LED lights.** (Although, there are some experts in landscaping and planted aquariums in general, who continue to use fluorescent tubes with excellent results).
- There are LED lamps that combine several colors (usually red, green, blue and white; RGBW), which allow to regulate them individually and highlight the colors of the fish and decoration.
- **The light intensity** must be **adequate** to the plants we have in the aquarium. Keep in mind that if we have a lot of light and few or no plants that use this resource, it will be the algae that can take advantage of it to grow.
- **The light** spectrum most commonly used by plants (specially plants with low and medium requirements) is **blue and red**. If you buy a light with red, green and blue LEDs and in a hypothetical case you only tank on the green light, this light will hardly be used by plants for photosynthesis (that is why plants are green, they reflect the wavelength of this color). On the other hand, there are algae that can use this color to proliferate.
- If your lamp is a **white LED** light, we are interested in a **color temperature between 6500 K and 7500 K (cold light).** This is better for plants. The lower the color temperature, the more yellow light, and the higher the temperature, the bluer.

- Additionally, it would be advisable to respect the natural conditions of the regions from which the fish and plants originate. Poorly regulated or adapted lighting leads to catastrophes. The maximum lighting period should be **12-14 hours**, corresponding to the daylight hours **of a tropical day.**
- You can also shift **lighting** times **to the evening,** if this is the time of day you spend the most time at home.

We will help you choose your lamp by giving you three different options, depending on the project you have in mind:

1. You have purchased an aquarium set, and it already has a lamp.
2. You are going to set up an aquarium without plants.
3. You are going to set up a low-medium tech aquarium with low to medium plant requirements, and you want adequate lighting. Later, in chapter 12, we will see what these concepts mean and talk more about plants.

There is a 4th option, which we will not deal with specifically in this book, which is to set up a high-tech aquarium, with plants of high requirements, with adequate lighting. In "Mejor Acuario", we believe that low-tech aquariums are more suitable for everyone, they are more natural and more self-sustainable.

Let's see what lighting you need in your particular case:

6.2 WHAT IS THE IDEAL LAMP FOR YOUR PROJECT?

1ST OPTION: YOU HAVE PURCHASED AN AQUARIUM SET INCLUDING LAMP

You already have it; you don't need another lamp! If this is your case, you have made a good and simple choice. Follow this path. **You can set up an aquarium without plants or with plants with low requirements**, as the lamps included in these sets are usually low wattage. If you are interested in having plants that are more demanding, you can read the third option. In this case, the only thing you have to do is remove the lid and the light that came with your aquarium and adapt a new one following the recommendations we are going to give you.

2ND OPTION: YOU NEED A LAMP AND YOU ARE NOT GOING TO HAVE PLANTS

Follow our general advice on lighting and based on this, buy the lamp you like the most, with LEDs in the colors you want and that best suits your budget and your aquarium. The lower the light intensity, the less likely algae will occupy the aquarium (although there are other important factors). **We recommend less than 30 lumens per liter of water.** That is if your aquarium has 100 liters, a lamp with approximately 2000 lumens will be sufficient. Don't forget that your fish need to differentiate between day and night. Establish a light and dark schedule. Between 7-9 hours of light per day is sufficient.

3RD OPTION: A LAMP FOR PLANTS WITH LOW/MEDIUM REQUIREMENTS

Get a lamp that has between 25-60 lumens per liter. It will need to be on for 7-9 hours a day. For example, if you have a 100-liter aquarium, you need a lamp that fits the length of your aquarium and has at least 2500 lumens; the closer to 6000 lumens, the better the plants will grow and the more variety you can have (in good conditions).

In Chapter 12, we will talk more about plants in aquariums and what light intensity you need depending on the type of plants you want to have.

Our recommendation for a low-medium tech planted aquarium

Our value for money recommendation for a Chihiro's Aquatic Studio white LED light from the A series or the A plus series. **Before buying,** to determine the best intensity for your needs, **you should read the section where we discuss plants in chapter 12.** Just to give you an idea, for 45 euros you could buy a 4500 lumens and 27W lamp on **AliExpress,** with a wide of variety of sizes and prices.

There are lamps designed for planted aquariums that combine colored LEDs and white LEDs, which are the latest on the market and are a great choice for plants with high fertilizer, light, and CO2 requirements. They can also be an excellent choice for low or medium-tech aquariums. They enhance the colors of the fish, although their price is also higher.

If you can invest more and want a higher-end lamp, within the **Chihiro's Aquatic Studio** brand, there **is the WRGB series,** where colored LEDs (blue, red, green) and white LEDs are combined. It's difficult to beat in terms of value for money by other brands at the time of writing, but there are many other brands on the market that can be a good choice.

This is going well!

We have already covered the three most important elements you need to start setting up your aquarium. You don't need to make a decision yet regarding what each one of them is going to be. You will be able to do that once you have finished reading the book.

7 THE SUBSTRATE: GRAVELS, SANDS AND NUTRITIVE SUBSTRATES

The substrate plays an important role in the decoration. Additionally, microscopic organisms and the roots of our plants will live in it.

There are a wide variety of substrates on the market. S<u>ome are inert</u>: they do **not interact with or modify the water parameters** and are useful for almost any type of project<u>, while others have specific characteristics and properties:</u> specific for plants, for shrimp tanks, to raise or lower the pH of the water, and so on.

Inert substrates are what we recommend using as a general rule. They are the most versatile, economical, require little care and maintenance, and can be used in almost all types of projects. Those of us who have been in this hobby for years continue to use them for all types of projects. **Although it is also possible to use "homemade" nutrient substrates with all the advantages and disadvantages that this entails.**

We have already done all the work for you, and we are going to explain, in a simple and summarized way, everything you need to know to set up aquariums for almost all types of fish, plants (both low-tech and high-tech), "neocarid shrimps", other invertebrates, small amphibians, etc.

Among the inert substrates we are going to discuss—gravels and sands—there is a wide variety of colors, so you can choose the color that you like the most.

Regarding brand recommendations for sands and gravels, there are many brands and many types of sands, all equally valid. We will provide some specific recommendations, but the objective is for you to be able to choose on your own.

7.1 GENERAL CHARACTERISTICS OF A GOOD SUBSTRATE

1. **Grain size.** A substrate with a medium grain size, between 1 and 5 millimeters thick, will allow the aquarium water flow to pass through it, providing oxygen and nutrients to the roots (in case you have plants) and will not allow anaerobic bacteria to accumulate. In the long term and without proper maintenance they could release toxins into the water.
2. **Grain shape.** We prefer the substrate to have rounded grains. Avoid using substrates for aquarium plants whose particles have sharp edges (it could also injure the fish).
3. **Porosity.** If the substrate also has a high porosity, it will have a greater capacity to harbor bacteria that help with water filtration.

4. **The composition should NOT be calcareous.** Calcareous substrates (such as certain sands formed by the remains of shells, corals or other calcium carbonate marine structures) increase the GH and pH in the aquarium water, making it difficult for plants to absorb CO2 and nutrients. In addition, by changing the water parameters, the water may no longer be ideal for your fish. Of course, there are specific ecosystems (such as an American cichlid biotope) where a substrate that increases GH and pH can be beneficial, but it is not recommended for general use.
5. **If you are going to have plants** and you are just starting, it is advisable to use an inert gravel or a substrate that allows nutrient exchanges. Another option that we will see later is to use an ordinary garden substrate, a universal substrate, the same as for terrestrial plants and cover it with a layer of 2-3 cm of gravel. This entails a risk, but it is not as great as we may think a priori.

7.2 RECOMMENDATIONS ACCORDING TO YOUR PARTICULAR PROJECT

We offer three options for you to choose the one that suits you best:

- One for aquariums without plants, with few plants **or** if we are not willing to make a major investment of money **or** want to make it as simple as possible.
- Another for aquariums with plants, whether they are plants with low requirements, or plants with high requirements **and** you are willing to make a greater economic investment.
- And finally, another option for aquariums with low **or** high requirement plants, which is economical but may have a higher risk.

All three options are compatible with all types of fish and invertebrate species.

UNPLANTED, WITH FEW PLANTS OR LESS ECONOMIC INVESTMENT

Use an inexpensive **inert substrate**, there are of all brands and all prices. To give you an idea, the average cost is about 10 euros per 100 liters of aquarium. We will also give you an option that we have in Spain and probably also other countries (doing a little search) with which for only 5 euros you can put substrate to aquariums up to 300 liters or more.

Inert substrates are those that do not interact with the aquarium water, and therefore do not modify the pH, GH, etc. parameters. **It is very simple, we have 2 types, gravels and sands,** which are usually silica (also quartz, which is the same).

A. THE GRAVES

The 1st option we offer you, is to put medium size aquarium gravel (1-5mm), the one you like the most. Aquarium gravel is an inert substrate. They are available in various grain size. **We recommend a medium size of between 1 and 5 mm, which will allow good water circulation and easy cleaning:** if we have plants, they allow a good water flow between the gaps between grain and grain, facilitating oxygen exchange, the supply of nutrients from the water column and avoiding stagnation and the appearance of toxins harmful to plants.

If it is going to be a planted aquarium, start by putting a layer of about 2-3 centimeters near the front, progressively increasing its thickness to about 4-5 centimeters at the back.

If you are not going to put plants. The thickness of the gravel layer is not so important. Decorate as you like. For example, a front layer of about 1-3 cm, growing progressively up to 3-5 cm at the back will give the aquarium a greater sense of depth. Leave the gravel on the bottom carefully so as not to scratch the glass.

The most common gravels on the market are those composed of silica. Make sure that the manufacturer indicates on the product that it is an inert gravel and that it is suitable for aquariums, you can choose the color you want.

"White quartz gravel" *"Black ceramic quartz gravel"*

B. THE SANDS

Another option for an inert substrate is silica sands, which **are inert substrates of smaller grain size.** Like gravels, they can be white or any other color. Aquarium sand has thicknesses of <0.5 to 1-2 mm.

Price-quality recommendations for sands in Spain:

- **If you are looking for a fine sand**: "Fine silica aquarium sand" from Verdecora.es. If you live in any other country, you will surely find other options, equal or better, in Google.
- **If you are looking for a sand with a slightly greater thickness, around 0.7 mm**: in Spain you can buy "*Sand AXTON de 25 kg*" for 5 euros at Leroy Merlin.

The latter is used for pool filters, but many colleagues have already tested them in their aquariums, they have tested the water, they are inert and the fish live in it without any problem. **Do not use just any silica sand you find on the market.** If you can't get this brand. Ask in your aquarium groups, google it and look at other guides on the internet, you will find opportunities just as good as this one!

Keep in mind that sands pose a challenge: the smaller the grain size of the sand the more compacted they become, resulting in poor water circulation, leading to stagnation. This generates anaerobic conditions in the substrate (no oxygen) and the production and possible release of toxins. They can also acquire a dirty appearance in a few weeks and favor the appearance of algae on their surface. **All this can be solved with proper weekly maintenance**, which could be summarized as: **weekly siphoning**, cleaning the remains of organic matter and removing and raising the compacted sand from the bottom to the surface (although this requires **more time of dedication**).

Also keep in mind that **silica sand is NOT optimal for the maintenance of plants** in the aquarium, especially because of these problems of water circulation and the accumulation of toxins.

PLANTED AQUARIUMS, WITH GREATER ECONOMIC INVESTMENT

"Example of a planted aquarium using JBL Manado"

We propose an intermediate option between inert and nutritive substrates. This option allows you **to set up a planted aquarium with any type of plant, whether they have low or high requirements**. The substrate will be rich in micronutrients and won't release macronutrients like nitrate and phosphate into the water column. Additionally, it will be capped with a non-inert layer that captures nitrate and phosphate from the water, making them available for plant roots.

At "Mejor Acuario", we have been recommending this substrate for years due to its excellent results. This substrate consists of three layers. The bottom layer comprises small volcanic rocks where plants can take root. On top of this, we place a layer of JBL Aquabasis enriched with micronutrients. Finally, we add a top layer of JBL Manado.

For an approximately 100-liter aquarium, combining these three substrate layers could cost around 50 euros. The cost approximately doubles with the aquarium's volume.

This substrate is suitable for nearly all species of fish and other animals you might consider placing in the aquarium. However, if you plan to have sensitive invertebrates such as neocaridinae, you need to exercise caution regarding certain metals. To avoid any issues, ensure that Aquabasis is well-sealed with a good layer of Manado following our recommendations (the manufacturer's guidelines are even stricter). Also, avoid disturbing the Aquabasis layer to prevent it from entering the water column

A. JBL MANADO

JBL Manado is one of the most commonly used freshwater aquarium substrates worldwide. It has a proven track record of successful use over many years. It can be used alone or together with **JBL Aquabasis**. Manado, a clay substrate, is not enriched with nutrients but naturally absorbs them from the water column over time. Like all clay substrates, it absorbs nitrogen, phosphorus, potassium, carbonates, and other micronutrients. The absorption rate depends on factors like the water's nutrient concentration, which can originate from the natural decomposition of organic matter or from fertilizers we add.

How to prepare Manado:

The first step is to wash the substrate. The manufacturer advises that JBL Manado may release calcium carbonate into the water. Washing it with hot water (boiling is not necessary) is crucial to prevent an increase in pH, GH, and KH. The product instructions clearly state this.

Depending on your location, you may or may not need to adjust this parameter. If you're using this substrate in very soft water (with low GH and low ppm), washing may not be necessary. *In Chapter 9, we will delve into hard and soft water and how to prepare aquarium water.*

Features of the JBL Manado

- **Brown or black color**.
- **Clayey texture**.
- Granule size ranges from **0.5mm and 2mm**.
- **Nutrient-free** substrate.
- Suitable for **fish, shrimp and other invertebrates, amphibians, etc.**
- Ideal for **bottom-dwelling fish** due to its smooth edges.
- **Long-lasting,** at least two years. Over time, the grains break down and form mud, resembling the disadvantage of compacted substrates like sands. Some aquarists have successfully maintained their plants and aquariums with this substrate for up to 9 years.

Advantages and disadvantages of the JBL Manado

ADVANTAGES

- **Does not** significantly **alter long-term water parameters.**
- **Absorbs and accumulates nutrients,** facilitating plant assimilation through their roots.
- **Allows good water circulation** due to its granule size.
- **Facilitates plant rooting.**
- **Maintains its integrity** over time.

DISADVANTAGES

- **Not a nutrient-rich substrate.**
- **Requires initial saturation,** resulting in rapid drops in nitrate and phosphate concentrations (especially when adding fertilizer) and necessitating increased attention during the first 2-4 weeks.
- **Less economical compared to gravels and sands.**
- **Initially, some grains float due to their low density,** making planting difficult.

How to saturate JBL Manado (in high tech fertilized aquariums)

How to Saturate JBL Manado (in high-tech fertilized aquariums): The substrate absorbs nutrients from the water, **reducing nitrate and phosphate** levels in the water. Over the first two weeks, nearly all the fertilized nutrients are "sequestered" by the substrate. To saturate the substrate, we primarily consider nitrate and phosphate levels. If, for instance, we add 1 mg/l of phosphate to the aquarium and within 24 hours, 0.5 mg/l disappears, it indicates a rapid decrease, particularly at the initial stages when plants have not yet developed. The substrate is absorbing the phosphate. We then test nitrate and phosphate levels and fertilize to reach 1 mg/l of phosphate and 10 mg/l of nitrate.

When the substrate stops absorbing nutrients, it is considered saturated. Care must be taken to avoid a rebound effect by not over-fertilizing once the saturation point is reached.

We believe that this substrate is an excellent option to start with planted aquariums. It allows us to learn how to fertilize before venturing into nutrient-rich substrates. Even after years of experience, we continue to use it.

How to combine JBL Manado

We will illustrate **how to combine JBL Manado with two other substrates: Aquabasis** and **volcanic stone** like JBL Volcano Mineral (there are similar substrates with cost-effective results).

B. JBL AQUABASIS PLUS

JBL Aquabasis is placed under the Manado. It is a natural clay that provides a nutritive support with micronutrients, releasing nutrients to the substrate and the plants roots. It is among the most commonly used substrates for planted aquariums, supplying almost all necessary **microelements and trace elements. However, it lacks nitrates, phosphates, or potassium so you need** to fertilize accordingly, especially in high tech set up or if you want to enrich potassium in your low-medium tech aquarium.

When using this nutrient substrate, **always** position it beneath the Manado, covering it completely with at least 3 cm of Manado to prevent micronutrient release. **Aquabasis doesn't wash out, and its layer should not be mixed with the Manado layer.**

C. VOLCANIC ROCK

JBL Volcano Mineral, a volcanic rock substrate, serves as the base substrate for the aforementioned ones. It **promotes water circulation** and enhances plant rooting.

We recommend seeking a substrate similar to JBL Volcano but at a lower cost. Depending on your location, you'll have various options available. **Look for substrates around 5 to 10 mm in size, similar to the one shown in the image.**

Tamaño 5-10 mm

D. FINAL SUBSTRATE ARRANGEMENT

We recommended a three-layer substrate, but it's not the sole option. Here are various combinations of these three substrates that you can choose based on your budget and personal preferences.

OPTION 1: Three-layer substrate, particularly recommended for heavily planted aquariums, both low and high tech. The numbers in the image may not align with ours as we believe using excessive substrate isn't necessary and isn't aesthetically pleasing.

1. A 1.5 - 2 cm layer of volcanic gravel (not shown in the picture).
2. On top, a 2-4cm layer of JBL Aquabasis
3. Finally, a 4-5 cm layer of JBL Manado.

OPTION 2: More budget-friendly and recommended for aquariums with lesser height for aesthetic reasons.

A single 4-6 cm layer of JBL Manado.

OPTION 3: A more cost-effective approach than the combination of the three layers, enhancing plant rooting.

1. **A layer of 1.5 - 2 cm of volcanic gravel**
2. **Finally, a 4-6 cm layer of JBL Manado.**

PLANTED AQUARIUMS, ECONOMICAL, BUT WITH HIGHER RISKS

Another option is to **utilize a standard garden substrate,** similar to what's used for terrestrial plants. While this entails some risk, it's not as significant as many aquarists may assume at first.

It's probable that using **only gravel** or sand in aquariums and attempting to **plant** might **not yield the desired results**. The plants may experience stunted growth and necessitate continuous substrate vacuuming to prevent the release of toxic substances.

Therefore, this stands as one of the potential solutions, which we'll elucidate below.

A. GENERAL CONSIDERATIONS

1. An **optimal** pH for the substrate would hover **around 6.6.**
2. **Turmoil in recently submerged terrestrial soils:** the chemical and biological instability of these substrates during **the initial 2 months** is well-documented. Various substrate traits can influence this instability, yet certain consistent events transpire. Oxygen supply is rapidly halted and swiftly consumed by bacteria and substrate chemicals. Notably, the bacteria eventually break down organic matter in the sediment under anaerobic conditions, releasing ammonium, hydrogen sulfide, and organic acids (acetic, formic, etc.) into the water from the substrate.
3. **How to avert the demise of our fish due to the release of toxic substances from the substrate?** We need to exercise **caution during the first few days and weeks,** as there might be an initial release of ammonium, metals, and more. This could be fatal to the fish or other creatures. Hence**, it's advisable to completely replace all the water in the aquarium at least once before introducing the fish.** You can also incorporate a water conditioner containing EDTA. If there's a suspicion that the substrate might contain pesticides, you could add activated carbon to the filter for the initial few weeks. Gradually, within the first 2 months, your substrate should attain stability.
4. **You can introduce the plants during the initial few days or weeks.** Furthermore, the roots of the plants release oxygen into their surroundings, oxygenating the substrate.
5. **Oxygenation of plant roots** and the surrounding area **benefits plants** in three ways: firstly, roots require oxygen for growth, sustenance, and nutrient absorption. Secondly, it counteracts toxins in the substrate.

Lastly, it can provide the aerobic environment needed for symbiotic fungi, which can enhance nutrient uptake by plants.

B. CHOOSING A SUBSTRATE

Both potting substrate and garden substrate can be utilized, but mixing them isn't advisable. As a general difference, it seems that fewer algae grow in potting media, but it might not be ideal in aquariums with soft water (GH <6-8). In such cases, periodic fertilization with "hard water nutrients" (Ca, Mg, K) might be necessary. For soft water aquariums, using garden substrate could be more suitable.

Several substrates have proven to be effective. Any potting soil from a local store will suffice—the same one used for potted plants (if you have one) is an option. It's advisable to avoid clay substrates from coastal areas near brackish water. Also, substrates from brands containing small Styrofoam balls floating on the surface should be avoided (although in this case, they can be removed before filling the aquarium). An ideal pH for the substrate would be around 6.6 (a neutral pH).

C. SETTING UP AN AQUARIUM WITH TERRESTRIAL SUBSTRATE?

There are many ways, but perhaps the simplest is as follow:

1. **Begin with a 2-3 cm thick layer of nutrient substrate at the tank's base.**
2. **Covering it with 2.5-3 cm of inert gravel, with a granule size of 1 to 4 mm.** The nutrient substrate should NOT be rinsed.
3. Add water to cover approximately 8 cm above the substrate. You can start planting.
4. Drain the murky water and refill the aquarium with clean water.
5. From this point onward, all components can be activated (water heater, filter, and lighting).
6. The next day, a water conditioner can be added. Any initial cloudiness should clear within 1 or 2 days.
7. After 4-6 weeks, you can begin introducing the first fish. Consider performing at least a partial water change before introducing the initial animals into the aquarium.

"Preparation of a Homemade Aquarium Substrate with Common Substrate"

We do **not** recommend **adding inorganic fertilizers** to substrates, as they can easily become toxic in submerged substrates. In planted aquariums, fish food acts as the fertilizer.

D. DOES THE SUBSTRATE DEGRADE OVER TIME?

Substrates devoid of plant roots and without gravel filtration do degrade over time. They accumulate organic matter, become anaerobic, and release toxins that can be lethal to our animals. Nutrient-rich and planted substrates can endure quite well for an extended period without gravel maintenance (such as vacuum cleaning).

The lifespan of the substrate depends on various factors, **including CO2 supplementation**. In a high-tech aquarium, plants can exhibit spectacular growth for about a year, which then gradually slows down. This phenomenon seems to occur even when plants are adequately fertilized with all essential nutrients. Conversely, in **aquariums without CO2** supplementation, **these substrates seem to last for years**, with continuous growth even after 4 or 5 years, if we allow.

This would be the result of a planted aquarium using this homemade substrate and a medium-tech light:

"A low-medium tech aquarium with homemade substrate, requiring minimal maintenance, without CO2 injection"

REMENBER THE KEY POINT ABOUT THE SUBSTRATE

Combining substrates with JBL Manado can yield satisfactory results in your plants if all other conditions are optimal. While it involves a more intricate initial setup, using potting soil covered by gravel can provide plants with all the necessary nutrients in a cost-effective manner.

However, a simpler approach, such as a gravel or sand substrate, is cost-effective, easy to maintain (in the case of gravel), and can still deliver acceptable results.

7.3 HOW MANY LITERS OF SUBSTRATE DO I NEED FOR MY AQUARIUM?

You've already decided on the substrate you want, for instance, a 4 cm layer of quartz or silica gravel, but you're unsure how much substrate you'll need for that layer in your aquarium. Well, the calculation is quite straightforward. Record the length, width, and height measurements of your aquarium, for instance, let's imagine your aquarium measures 120 x 50 x 40 cm.

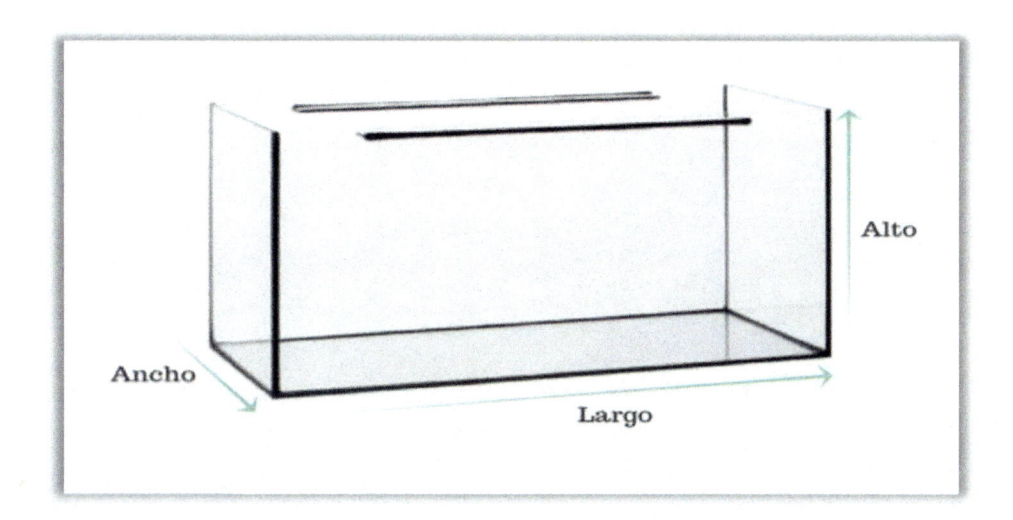

Replace the height of the aquarium (in this case, 40 cm) with the thickness of the substrate layer you desire. Let's say we want a 4 cm thick layer:

120 x 50 x 4 cm = 24000 cm3 = 24 Liters. You would require a total of 24 liters of substrate to achieve a 4 cm thick layer if your aquarium had these dimensions.

Another step closer!

The choice of substrate is one of the most important factors for healthy plant development in your aquarium, consequently preventing algae from proliferating.

8 SUMMARY: THE EQUIPMENT YOUR ECOSYSTEM REQUIRES

Now, you know what you need: a tank, a filter with filter media, a lamp, and substrate. In this section, we'll delve into what else you need, elaborating further in the subsequent chapters. Towards the end of the book, in "Appendix 2," along with budgeting guidelines, you'll find some examples of specific equipment.

Below, you'll find a list encompassing everything you need, presented this way in case it's your first time setting up an aquarium, making it your shopping list:

List of essential equipment, materials, and products every aquarium need:

<u>Essential</u>

- Tank
- Filter and filter media
- Lighting
- Substrate
- Thermometer
- Water conditioner
- Nitrate or other test strips* (Best to use "drop" test).
- Bacteria for aquarium cycling*.
- PPM or TDS METER
- Power strip with at least 6 sockets (with extension cable of the appropriate size depending on the aquarium´s placement) and timers
- Wifi-enabled power strip (can replace the previous one)

Items marked with * are not mandatory but might be useful.

<u>Situational:</u>

- <u>Heater:</u> essential for warm water or tropical aquariums. Depending on your region's climate and your aquarium's location, it might be recommended.
- <u>Fan:</u> for cooling the water in summer if your aquarium water exceeds 29-30ºC.
- <u>Aerator or bubble pump:</u> crucial for proper gas exchange and water oxygenation (generally recommended).

<u>Optional</u>

- <u>Inlet and outlet glass pipettes</u> for external filters: for aesthetic reasons, to replace the default ones that come with the filters (images available in Annex 2).
- <u>Pre-filter:</u> it is optional but cost-effective and highly recommended, especially for aquariums with plants or if you have young fish or shrimp.

Additionally, for planted aquariums <u>with plants with high requirements</u>:

- Plant pruning kit.
- Fertilizers.
- Nitrate and phosphate test.
- CO2 Bottle
- CO2 Regulator
- CO2 Diffuser

8.1 WHAT DON'T YOU NEED FOR YOUR AQUARIUM?

We've provided specific recommendations on what you need regarding filters, filter materials, substrate, etc., and we'll explore the remaining equipment in the book's second part. It's **very important, to avoid overspending, to purchase equipment and products with a clear objective in mind**. For instance:

We emphasize the filter and filter material's quality because if you don't invest in a proper filter, you might need to buy another one soon. When it comes to purchasing a water heater, we suggest: "buy any heater" because there are many affordable options that can yield good results. In general, all heaters work well, even those priced at 9-12 euros on AliExpress.

We also discourage purchasing anti-algae products, **water quality products**, or any other product aside from water conditioner and a bacteria canister. **These are unnecessary and don't significantly enhance water quality**.

Certainly, you can augment your equipment with any material you desire, but our goal is to recommend only what truly matters.

Many of us who ventured into the aquarium hobby without proper guidance have bought numerous unnecessary products that ended up unused or discarded. We've also bought inappropriate or low-quality products that needed quick replacement.

Seize this opportunity! Learn from these mistakes and make informed choices!

PART 2

"THE TECHNIQUE"

When we mention "the technique" we refer to:

"The aquarist's ability to manage the parameters of their ecosystem and achieve and maintain a stable water quality.

9 THE IMPORTANCE OF WATER

Every chapter in this book orbits around a central objective: water quality within the ecosystem. Quality water denotes that the substances dissolved within it and other parameters, like temperature, are optimal for the life of the animals inhabiting it. In this chapter, you will comprehend why this aspect is crucial and where you'll garner extensive knowledge to attain it.

Water stands as the paramount element of your aquarium. For our animals, water holds the same significance as the air we breathe does for us. If the air we breathe were toxic, it would stifle us, induce illness, and curtail our life expectancy. A similar scenario unfolds in our aquariums. Let's examine the following diagram:

DIAGRAM DEPICTING CAUSES AND CONSEQUENCES OF WATER QUALITY IN OUR AQUARIUM

Modifiable factors: filtration, natural plants, water changes, overpopulation, etc.

Water quality and its parameters: GH, pH, temperature, toxic substances, oxygen, etc.

Issues: Diseases, cloudy water, toxic water, algae, etc.

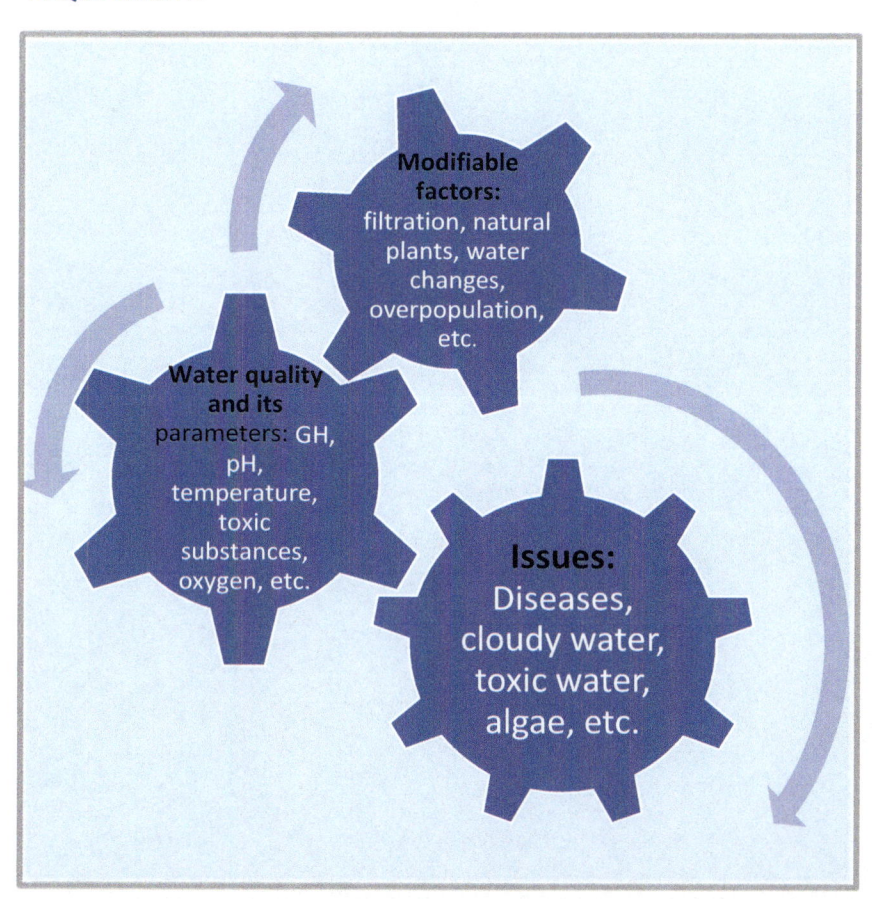

"The quality of water (clean and devoid of toxins) and its appropriate parameters (GH, pH, temperature...)" are outcomes resulting from the individual contribution of each facet of the ecosystem within our control: "modifiable factors" (effective filtration, utilization of natural plants to enhance filtration, adjustments of parameters and water conditioning during changes, control of overpopulation...).

Another way to express it, **poor water quality is a result of:**

- **Inadequate GH in the water added during changes for our species of fish**, or we have neglected the conditioner.
- **Infrequent or nonexistent water changes** (essential for eliminating toxins that our ecosystem cannot handle).
- **Infrequent removal of organic matter remnants** (excess food, feces, deceased fish, dead leaves, and stems...).
- **Inadequate filtration,** causing the accumulation of ammonia and nitrites (recall that ammonium and nitrites are more toxic than nitrates).
- Utilization of **artificial decor without leveraging the filtration potential of natural plants.**
- **Inadequate** dissolved **oxygen levels** in the water.
- Substrate or decor that alters water parameters and/or releases toxic substances into the water.

- And various other causes we have explored and will continue to explore throughout this book.

The consequence of poor "water quality" are all the "problems" in our aquarium: diseases, stress, fish jumping out of the tank, short life expectancy in our animals, algae, turbid water and almost everything you can think of. Once these issues arise, they can further degrade water quality, perpetuating the cycle and devastating our ecosystem if timely intervention does not occur.

We firmly believe, and this belief has proven effective with fellow enthusiasts: **the most vital aspect is proactive problem prevention** through comprehension and adept management of each "modifiable factor" within our ecosystem. Focusing on individual remedies for each issue as they arise takes a back seat, as **a problem typically begets others, and if we do not address the root cause, it will resurface.**

For instance, combatting algae doesn't entail manual removal, hydrogen peroxide, glutaraldehyde, darkness, water changes, or other methods (some quite inventive) one might stumble upon online. Instead, it involves addressing the underlying factors predisposing its growth, such as nutrient imbalances or subpar filtration.

Let's look at the example of a fellow who shared how their Goldfish were falling ill...

We met Manu through an aquarium hobby group. One day, he shared a picture of one of his goldfish, the image was similar to the one below:

"Sick Goldfish with white spot"

He told us that he had recently introduced another goldfish into his 200-liter aquarium. The aquarium was equipped with a 25-watt LED light, a white quartz gravel substrate, some "Eleocharis" and some planted "Echinodorus" and an internal filter with a theoretical flow rate of 1000 liters per hour and a capacity for filter material of approximately 2 liters. The filter contained ceramic biofiltration cylinders (he was uncertain about the brand) and foam sponge. He already had 9 adult Goldfish and a week ago, he added the tenth one.

The problem: 3 days after the arrival of the new goldfish into the aquarium, it was found dead in the morning with white spots on its body, as seen in the image. Manu removed it out of the water, not thinking much of it. After 2 days, another goldfish, which had been in the aquarium for more than 2 years, started displaying white spots too.

This condition is known as white spot disease, caused by a parasite that infests fish and creates sores on their skin, leading to over-infection by other bacteria or fungi and eventual death. Likely, the newly introduced fish was already sick, succumbed to the illness, and transmitted it to the others. Moreover, the aquarium water was slightly cloudy, a condition that was quite common, as he explained.

Specific treatments exist for this disease that can effectively cure an infected fish. However, what facilitates the transmission and contagion of these parasites and other diseases is often the pre-existing weakness of the fish, primarily due to poor water quality: unstable or inappropriate parameters such as temperature, GH, pH, excess ammonium, and more. Inadequate feeding and inappropriate decoration for a species that is prone to skin lesions can also contribute.

We won't delve into the specific treatment of this particular fish; you can find numerous guides on treating this disease (it's important to cross-reference the information and rely on trusted sources).

In this case, it's evident that the arrival of a parasite in the aquarium via the new goldfish triggered the problem, but the other fish likely fell ill due to poor water quality.

The water in his aquarium had a slightly cloudy-greenish hue. Considering the size of the fish and the amount of organic waste they produced, it's recommended to have at least 30-40 liters of water for each goldfish.

For an aquarium like his, with that number of fish, it would also be advisable to have at least 1 liter of high-quality biological filter media per 100 liters. The flow was acceptable, but given that the theoretical flow is usually less than the actual flow, having at least 6-7 times the volume of the aquarium would be prudent.

Upon testing for ammonium, the concentration was 0.6 mg per liter. The ideal is 0, and a concentration of 1 to 2 mg per liter can be lethal within a few days.

The solution: To gradually change the filter material to 1.5 liters of biological material (no more would fit in the filter), eliminating mechanical filtration, and individually treating two more fish that had begun to develop the disease with a specific treatment. Changing the filter was highly recommended, and if ammonium values increased again, that would be the next step. For now, the problem was resolved.

The outcome was that despite maintaining overstocking in his aquarium, a change and adjustment of the filter media resolved the ammonium issue. Ten days after implementing the changes, the water showed ammonium concentrations beyond the sensitivity of the test. As the new filter media was colonized by bacteria from the old media, he maintained low ammonium concentrations with frequent water changes.

What triggered the problem was the introduction of a sick fish into the aquarium, but the contagion to the rest was because their fish were tolerating toxic concentrations of ammonium due to:

- Using the same filter media for >5 years, which had declined in its ability to support nitrifying bacteria.
- It's crucial to invest a bit more in high-quality biological filtration material.
- The filter had a very limited filter media capacity (2 liters) for a 200-liter aquarium with 9 goldfish, and the flow rate was at the lower end of the recommended range. Additionally, it was also occupied by a foam sponge.
- The aquarium was overstocked.

Conclusion: If the fish are falling ill, the solution doesn't merely lie in treating them with antibiotics or other specific remedies. In most cases, water quality is a major factor predisposing fish to diseases.

A curiosity: "Swim bladder" is a common issue in goldfish, causing buoyancy problems due to obstruction in the air inlet and outlet of their swim bladder, making regulation impossible. **The primary trigger** is often inappropriate feeding, but poor water quality usually **predisposes** fish to this condition.

The approach to achieving ideal water for those starting a project from scratch involves following our step-by-step recommendations regarding equipment and aquarium management. For those who already have an aquatic ecosystem, it may involve interventions like adjusting the filter, filter material, substrate, lighting, and cleaning, or more direct actions like regulating parameters such as GH, pH, water changes, temperature, and oxygenation.

*A final recommendation is to **avoid using natural waters from rivers**, ponds, lakes, or rain, as they can introduce problems related to **contamination** and suspended particles into the aquarium, along with potential **microorganisms** that could infect or parasitize our animals.*

9.1 WATER PARAMETERS: ADJUSTING GH, KH AND PH

We'll start with adjustments directly related to the water. The key parameters to consider when preparing aquarium water are GH, pH, and KH. **The primary factor influencing and modifying these parameters in your aquarium water is the water added during each water change,** as these parameters remain relatively constant without intervention.

CONCEPTS: GH, KH AND PH.

A. WATER HARDNESS. DEGREES OF TOTAL HARDNESS (DGH).

Freshwater fish typically require low to medium hardness, with GH between 2-15 (for almost all fish). General hardness or degrees of total hardness (dGH or °GH) is a measure of divalent metal ion concentration, **meaning:**

GH = calcium ions (Ca2+) + magnesium (Mg2+) dissolved in water

Technically, to **speak of water hardness is to speak of the calcium and magnesium concentrations** of the water, with calcium generally dominating. And generally, but not always, the concentrations of bicarbonate, Cl, K, and S are associated with water hardness. Thus, **hard water contains large amounts of Ca, HCO3, Cl, K, Mg, and S** (the plant nutrients of hard water).

B. CARBONATE HARDNESS. DEGREES OF CARBONATE HARDNESS (DKH).

Carbonate hardness grades measure temporary or carbonate hardness, acting as a pH buffer. it opposes the pH variation. A recommended range for kH is between 3 and 10. Generally, **higher GH values correspond to higher KH values.** For us:

KH = calcium carbonate (CaCO$_3$) + magnesium carbonate (MgCO)$_3$

C. WATER PH

PH indicates the water´s acidity degree, balancing the acid and alkaline components present in the water:

- pH = 7 = neutral water
- pH > 7 = basic water
- pH > 7 = acidic water

D. ANOTHER IMPORTANT CONCEPT: HARD OR SOFT WATER

Based on what we have just said, in other words:

Hard water, opposed to soft water, as a higher concentration of magnesium and calcium minerals. In other words, <u>hard water has a high GH</u>, which is usually associated with a high KH.

IDEAL GH, KH AND PH PARAMETERS

There are no universally ideal values for <u>all</u> fish, plants and invertebrates, as each species has its recommended parameter range. However, some values are likely to fall within the ideal range for most animals (and plants). These can be useful for setting up a community aquarium:

What are these ideal (or close to ideal) parameters for most species?

- GH between 5-12
- pH between 6.5-7.5
- Temperature between 22ºC and 24ºC for warm water or tropical fish (in summer try to keep it below 28-30ºC).
- For cold water fish like Carassius or goldfish, between 10 and 26ºC (depending on season). Always check species-specific requirements!

These are general recommendations, but **it is best to adjust your water parameters based on the species in your aquarium:**

HOW TO CHOOSE IDEAL PARAMETERS FOR YOUR SPECIFIC AQUARIUM?

1. Research each species of animal in your aquarium, noting down the ideal GH and temperature range for each species.
2. **Document each species and its ideal GH and temperature range**.
3. **Select a GH value within the ideal range for all species** or as close as possible, **and do the same for temperature.**
4. If you have incompatible species, consider finding separate homes for them.

Also, **keep in mind that plants require minimum GH conditions**; a GH of **at least 4-5** is necessary for them, and up to a GH of 20 would be ideal.

HIGHLIGHTS OF THIS SECTION:

One of the reasons why many aquarists neglect measuring or attending to their water parameters is the complexity of adjusting them. Multiple tests are needed to measure each parameter individually, requiring water mixing and rechecking for accuracy. **After years of experience, we've discovered a VERY EFFECTIVE, affordable, and simple METHOD to achieve this crucial adjustment. We're eager to share this approach with you.**

9.2 WATER PARAMETERS: FORGET ABOUT GH, KH AND PH

Now that you know what these terms mean and how to determine the parameters your species need: you won't need to know anything more about them! By following this guide, you'll likely never need to worry about GH, KH, pH, or use tests. In any case, you won't need them now.

But what are ppm or parts per million? For us, ppm refers to the milligrams (mg) of solutes (calcium and magnesium) dissolved in 1 liter of water, which **is equivalent to water hardness or GH. A simple and practical way to view it is:** a concentration of 100 to 200 ppm or mg/l is equal to the ideal GH conditions for most of our fish, invertebrates, amphibians, and plants. **Here's a summary:**

100-200 ppm = GH of 6 - 12º / KH of 3 - 10º / pH of 6,5 - 7,5

What do we need? We only need a **"PPM METER or TDS METER** (they are the same)," which **helps us approximate**, with sufficient precision (following the instructions we'll provide), **the GH of your tap water, osmosis, or bottled water**. Therefore, **a ppm or TDS meter helps us adjust the GH or hardness of the water (before adding it to the aquarium**), **ensuring our animals have an ideal and stable hardness with each water change**. It instantly estimates the GH without the need for testing. To use it, you'll need to convert GH to ppm (parts per million) or mg/L, which is what our "ppm meter" measures and vice versa.

Basics of the method: **before adding water to the aquarium** (tap, osmosis, or bottled water), it has **a GH directly related to the number of parts per million in the water (ppm)**. Generally, the higher the GH, **the higher the KH and pH**. Conversely, lower GH results in lower KH and pH. However, this may vary, especially in localities with water from desalination plants or buildings with water softeners. For example:

When preparing water in a container before adding it to the aquarium during a water change, setting it to 165 ppm (for example), the GH will be 10. With very high probability, your KH will range between 2 and 10, and your pH will be between 6.5 and 7.5. If you increase the GH or ppm for a particular fish species, it will also raise the KH and pH. (Species requiring a higher GH for ideal conditions will also need a higher KH and pH.)

GH	mg/litre	Considered as
0 - 3	0 - 50	Soft
3 - 6	50 - 100	Moderately Soft
6 - 12	100 - 200	Slightly Hard
12 - 18	200 - 300	Moderately hard
18 - 25	300 - 450	Hard
Over 25	Over 450	Very Hard

We leave you a table with other equivalences. You can find online **a calculator that convert ppm to GH and vice versa.**

For a community aquarium, **a value of 130 ppm (GH = 7.8)** might be suitable. For a community aquarium, most freshwater animal species available in stores will thrive at 130 ppm, including Neocaridina shrimp, other invertebrates, and some small amphibians like frogs.

Though it's ideal to know the right ppm for your specific aquarium. Let's now learn how to do that.

HOW TO CHOOSE THE PPM VALUE FOR YOUR AQUARIUM WATER CHANGES?

Follow these steps to choose an ideal GH if you haven't already:

1. Research each species of animals in your aquarium, both fish and other animals.

2. **Note down the GH range for each species.**
3. **Choose a GH value that falls within the ideal range for all** species or as close as possible, and make a note of it.
4. **If you have incompatible species, try to relocate them to another of your aquariums or to another aquarist's aquarium.**

And then:

5. **Once you know the ideal GH, use the equivalence table or the GH to ppm calculator to determine the ideal ppm for the water to be added during each water change.**

Attention, please, the ppm meter is only used to calculate the GH before adding the water to the aquarium. Once the water is in the aquarium, other dissolved substances can increase the ppm values without affecting GH or hardness. **(Do not use the ppm meter in the aquarium water to adjust GH; it won't work.)** Therefore, **to adjust the GH of our aquarium water to the desired value, we'll do it through water changes.**

HOW TO ADJUST THE PPM IN WATER CHANGES TO ACHIEVE THE DESIRED GH IN THE AQUARIUM?

The first step is to *get a PPM or TDS METER*. This device measures dissolved particles in water. **IT IS THE ONLY TOOL YOU WILL NEED TO ADJUST YOUR WATER PARAMETERS.**

A ppm meter typically costs between 7 and 15 euros. You can find them very affordably on AliExpress and slightly more expensive but still very accessible on Amazon. The only maintenance required is to change the battery every few years. Rarely, depending on usage, they may need calibration.

HOW TO USE THE METER TO ADJUST THE PARAMETERS?

In chapter 14, we will learn how to determine the GH our animals and therefore our aquarium, need.

Let's imagine that, due to our fish or other animals' characteristics, we need a concentration of 130 ppm (GH=7.8):

First, procure a sufficiently large container to blend the necessary liters of water for your aquarium's water change. If your aquarium holds 100 liters, ideally, the container should have a capacity of at least 30 liters.

1º Measure the ppm of your tap water. If they fall within the optimal range for your animals, excellent! You can use your tap water for your aquarium, eliminating the need for osmosis or bottled water. However, in most cases, this is NOT the situation.

2º If the ppm of your tap water is lower than you need, you'll need to augment it. Visit the nearest supermarket and search for water with the highest hardness available, implying strong mineralization, a high calcium and magnesium content, a high number of particles per million, or a high GH. Look for the most economical option. Gradually add strongly mineralized bottled water to your tap water in the blending container until you achieve the desired ppm concentration.

An even more convenient and likely cost-effective alternative is to **purchase salts** that increase the GH and KH of the water, such as "JBL Aquadur salts." **Remember:** DO NOT directly introduce salts into your aquarium water or adjust the ppm during water changes directly in the aquarium water.

3º. In case the ppm of your tap water exceeds the required ppm, you'll need to decrease them. Look for the most affordable **bottled water with the least mineralization you can find**; in other words, low hardness, low GH, low calcium and magnesium content, or low ppm. If you have access to osmosis water, use it and blend it with your tap water until you **reach the target ppm**.

Combine water with higher hardness with water of lower hardness in the container, gradually measuring with the ppm meter until you achieve the necessary liters at the desired ppm for your aquarium, approximately. Once accomplished, proceed to the 4th step.

4º. Introduce the water into the aquarium. Even if you've previously filled the aquarium and even if the fish are **already present, don't worry**. Determine the ideal GH for your animals. Once you know this, execute the usual weekly water changes of 20-30% of the aquarium water. However, now, the water you add during each change must be adjusted to achieve the ideal GH for your aquarium. **Week after week, the water hardness will transition progressively (as animals cannot tolerate abrupt changes) until it aligns with what you desire.**

A tip: prepare water for the weekly changes in bottles—some with high GH water and others with low GH water.

Each week, utilize these bottles for your aquarium's water changes. Afterward, refill them, add the "water conditioner" (which we will soon elaborate on), and store them until the following week. When the time comes for the water change, you'll have the water ready and conditioned.

In summary: Use a container to combine tap water, osmosis water, bottled water, or artificial GH and KH salts according to your specific case until you achieve the ideal ppm concentration for your fish (typically around 100-200 ppm). Then, perform a water change for your aquarium using this prepared water.

And there you have it! The first time is the most difficult, and then the problems are over!

RECOMMENDATIONS FOR ADJUSTING THE PPM OF YOUR AQUARIUM WATER

- If you're in the initial stages of setting up the aquarium and there are NO animals inside, and the cycling hasn't commenced yet because you've recently filled the tank, you can adjust the ppm by mixing inside the aquarium until you reach your desired level. Then, add the "water conditioner" (we'll explain what this is shortly).
- If your aquarium is already cycling or is a mature one with fish and plants, and you aim to get the water just right for your animals, capitalize on your weekly maintenance routine. During the 20-30% weekly water changes, use the water mix you've prepared at your target GH or ppm. Mix the water in a container before adding it to the tank.
- **Avoid abrupt changes in water parameters, as animals cannot tolerate sudden shifts**. Stick to your routine of weekly water changes, but now, with each change, add water with the ideal ppm for your fish. Gradually, over a few weeks, the GH will decrease and align with the ideal conditions.
- **IMPORTANT:** **The ppm meter should only be used to calculate the GH** of tap, osmosis, or bottled water, or when you're preparing the mixture in a container. **Do not use it to calculate the GH of the water already in your aquarium.**

Why? Because there are other dissolved particles in the aquarium water, such as nitrates (among others), which are not present in tap or bottled water (it's normal for nitrates to start appearing in a cycled aquarium), and these particles also increase the ppm even if the GH remains stable.

We emphasize: DO NOT FORGET THAT THE PPM OF THE WATER INSIDE THE AQUARIUM IS NOT EQUAL TO GH OR WATER HARDNESS. **If the water you add to your aquarium every week has 130 ppm (GH=7.8), the hardness of your aquarium water is GH=7.8, even if the ppm of the aquarium water is 250 ppm** (as long as everything inside the aquarium, mainly substrate and decoration, is inert, as we recommended before). This is because there are also other substances dissolved in the water (such as nitrates and many more) that increase the ppm without affecting the GH.

If your aquarium is already established, even if you've had it for years and your fish are "surviving," look up the ideal GH and temperature for the species you have on Google. Likely, if the conditions aren't appropriate, you may have experienced occasional losses, some fish might have fallen ill, and others might not be meeting the life expectancy of their species, etc. (best-case scenario).

If these parameters are suitable, and you're still facing issues, in the filtration chapter, we've discussed another frequent cause of these problems. We'll also explore other likely causes later on.

Follow our recommendation: **start doing things right! Enhance your fish's quality of life.** There are experienced aquarists who, despite years of experience, have never considered the importance of these parameters in their aquariums. In many of these cases, their animals and plants barely survive, struggle with health issues, and don't meet their life expectancy.

If you're reading this book and putting it into practice, you've just resolved this issue once and for all: CONGRATULATIONS!

OTHER TIPS

When pouring water into the aquarium, direct it over a dish or bowl to ensure a smooth flow into the tank without disturbing the gravel, decorations, or plants.

Leave approximately 3-4 centimeters of space without water. This prevents overflow in case you need to reach into the tank for any reason.

KEY IDEAS ON GH, KH AND PH

During regular water changes, always add water adjusted to the ppm corresponding to the ideal GH for your fish. Before adding it to the aquarium, use a "conditioner." The ppm dissolved in your aquarium will never match the water you add each week; it will always be higher.

Adjusting these parameters is a simple and cost-effective way to enhance water quality for your species. Forget about complex drug treatments and focus on water quality. Many aquarium hobbyists overlook monitoring their aquarium's water parameters. We strongly discourage this practice as it leads to suffering, disease, and shortened life expectancy for our animals. ***It's incredibly easy to get it right with our method!***

Remember, once again... We apologize for the repetition...

The water in your aquarium will always have a higher ppm than the water you change every week during maintenance. For example, if you're adding water with a concentration of 130 ppm, it's likely that your aquarium usually measures between 200 - 270 ppm. This is normal **because other dissolved substances in the aquarium water increase the ppm, though they do NOT affect the GH.** *In other words, if tap water measures 300 ppm, its GH is 18. However, if your aquarium water reads 300 ppm, the GH will* **NOT** *be 18; it will be lower. Ppm is only useful for calculating the GH of tap, osmosis, or bottled water, or when you're preparing it with GH and KH salts. It is not useful for calculating the GH of your aquarium water.*

When we discuss maintenance, we'll provide more practical tips and additional ideas on how to conduct water changes.

9.3 ONE MORE THING BEFORE ADDING WATER TO YOUR AQUARIUM

WATER CONDITIONER

Besides the ppm or TDS meter, another essential product for adjusting your aquarium's water parameters is a high-**quality** "water conditioner." Its role is to **remove chlorine and chloramines from the water before adding it to the aquarium**. Chlorine would eliminate the bacteria in our aquarium and disrupt the "nitrogen cycle" (we'll explain this shortly). We recommend "PRIME by SEACHEM." While **there are other quality options, we suggest choosing one that contains EDTA.**

When should you use it? ALWAYS. When setting up the aquarium for the first time, you'll need to use it. Additionally, use it in the water you'll use for water changes. Apply it a few minutes or a few hours before (according to the manufacturer's recommendations) to allow it to take effect.

Conditioners have the capability to eliminate chlorine, heavy metals, and, in high concentrations, nitrates, nitrites, and ammonium.

This is not optional. You may have read that leaving the bottle open allows chlorine to evaporate. Disregard this notion; nowadays, tap water contains chloramines and other substances that do not evaporate.

Invest in a good conditioner. **In the case of a better aquarium, we recommend and use "PRIME by Seachem."** It has yielded excellent results for us and is economical: **with 50 ml and at approximately 7-10 euros, you'll have enough conditioner to last at least 2-3 years for a 100-liter aquarium. It's one of the most cost-effective products for your aquarium.**

Follow the manufacturer's instructions for use, typically involving adding a few drops to the **water at least 1 hour before** introducing it into the aquarium. However, 10-15 minutes may suffice.

While it's unlikely, some osmosis water may NOT completely remove chloramines. Our recommendation is **NOT to save a few drops and use the conditioner in osmosis water as well. It's also necessary to use it in bottled water,** as it contains chloramines.

9.4 WATER PARAMETERS: TEMPERATURE ADJUSTMENT

A common misconception among aquarists is to equate "cold water" with "any temperature." Warm water or tropical fish typically thrive at consistent temperatures throughout the year, with only a few degrees of fluctuation due to seasonal changes. On the other hand, **cold-water fish generally hail from regions where water temperatures can range from 10ºC to 28-30ºC.**

In ideal conditions, **tropical fish usually inhabit temperatures between 22ªC and 26ºC.** Conversely, some common cold-water fish, such as the "Carassius auratus" family (which includes goldfish), ideally thrive between 10ºC and 29ºC, depending on the season.

When we refer to a temperature range of 10ºC to 29ºC, we are considering **gradual temperature changes across the seasons.** Temperature fluctuations exceeding one degree within 24-48 hours can induce physiological stress, making our fish, whether warm or cold water, weak and susceptible to illness.

A brief note about "Carassius auratus" (the orange cold water fish): We've all seen round glass fish tanks and 5-liter plastic fish bowls with an orange fish inside, assuming all a fish needs is water and food to survive. However, the "goldfish" requires much more than that for a healthy life: clean water free of ammonium, a neutral pH (6.5 to 7.5), water with a GH of 5 to 15º, and aquariums ranging from 120-200 liters (goldfish and other carp are pond fish), among other factors, just like any other animal.

Temperature is a crucial factor in planted aquariums as well, given that very few plant species can tolerate temperatures below 18ºC or above 30ºC in optimal conditions. During summer, in regions where temperatures rise, and aquarium water temperature exceeds 30ºC, problems may arise with fish and plants. **Beyond 32ºC, some animals and plants might not survive the summer.**

In summary: **The temperature required for your aquarium will depend on the animals and plants you want to keep in it.** Very simple:

- Most tropical fish commonly found in stores thrive at around 24ºC (between 22ºC and 26ºC). Strive to keep them below 30ºC and above 18-20ºC.
- Cold-water fish of the "Carassius auratus" family tolerate temperatures between 10ºC and 29ºC well. **"Carassius auratus" family can tolerate temperatures slightly below 10ºC in ponds during the winter.**
- Whether your fish are warm or cold water, temperature changes should be gradual, never exceeding 1-2ºC in less than 24-48 hours.
- For aquarium plants, a temperature above 18ºC and up to 29ºC (in summer) would be ideal.

In Chapter 14, "The Inhabitants of the Aquarium," you'll learn how to adjust the water temperature based on the fish and other animals in your aquarium.

THERMOMETER

Every aquarium needs a thermometer, whether it's a cold-water or warm-water tank. **If you have a heater, don't solely rely on its thermostat; include a thermometer.** Place the thermometer away from the heater (proper water circulation makes this less critical).

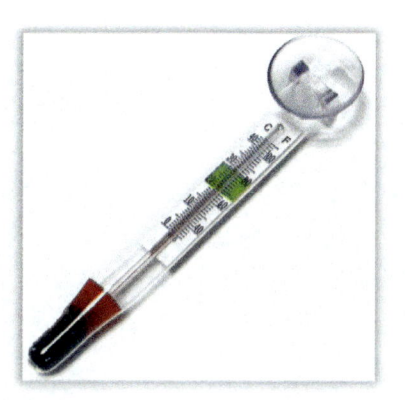

Which one is the best? Choose the one you like the most and is the most economical. At "Mejor Acuario", we recommend the classic type—it's reliable and aesthetically pleasing. It's priced at around 2 to 4 euros, depending on where you purchase it.

Let's illustrate a common problem:

You have a heater in your aquarium set at 24ºC, but the thermometer reads 26ºC. This indicates that your heater's thermostat needs adjustment. Regardless, trust **the thermometer's reading as the real temperature.** Adjust the heater temperature to 23 or 22 ºC until the thermometer reflects the desired temperature.

THE AQUARIUM HEATER - DO I NEED A HEATER FOR MY AQUARIUM?

The answer is straightforward:

- If you don't reside in a tropical climate with a minimum water temperature of 20ºC and you want to keep tropical-water fish, the answer is **YES**—you need a heater.
- If you plan to keep cold-water fish in the aquarium, and your home's winter temperature doesn't fall below the tolerance range of these fish, you do **NOT** need one.

- If you intend to have plants in your aquarium and your home experiences winter temperatures below 18ºC, we recommend you a heater.

We recommend **not overspending on the heater.** For approximately 8-12 euros, you can purchase a heater ranging from 100-300 watts on AliExpress, suitable for aquariums of about 100-300 liters. They function effectively and are also available at similar prices in other stores. If you invest a bit more, it might provide you with added peace of mind, allowing you to regularly verify that the thermostat's indicated temperature matches the actual water temperature.

Place the heater where it looks aesthetically pleasing and where there's water flow (this isn't an issue with adequate and well-positioned filtration). Always connect the heater, as it includes an automatic thermostat that will turn it on and off based on the water's temperature.

The watts your heater needs **are 0.75 - 1.5w per liter of the aquarium.** For instance, **for a 100L aquarium, a heater between 75-150 watts would be suitable. In very cold rooms, it's advisable to use at least 1w per 100L.** Only turn on the heater 5-10 minutes after placing it in the aquarium; a sudden temperature change can cause the glass to break.

HOW TO LOWER THE TEMPERATURE OF MY AQUARIUM IN SUMMER? THE FAN

This is a common concern in regions experiencing very hot summers. Do not overlook this aspect, as there are numerous cases of hobbyists losing parts of their plants and animals due to summer heat. Fortunately, we have a simple and affordable solution.

For those living in regions where temperatures soar to 35-40ºC (outdoors) during summer, this is crucial. It's common to find aquarium water temperatures exceeding 32ºC. **Ideally, keep it below 28ºC (in general). How? Simple, with a fan. Additionally, other measures such as avoiding direct sunlight (preferably all year round),** using LED lights, or leaving the aquarium uncovered can also help.

There are other options, but we won't delve into them due to their cost and complexity. **Choose a fan (or a set of fans) that covers at least most of your aquarium's width or half its length.** For example, if your aquarium is 60 cm long and 40 cm wide, a fan measuring about 25-30 cm should suffice. Such a fan can typically lower your aquarium's temperature by 4ºC. If needed, you can opt for a larger fan or add a second one.

Connect the fan to a timer and adjust the on/off times based on the aquarium temperature: every 24 hours, monitor the aquarium temperature and tweak the switch-on times, ensuring the water temperature stays below 30ºC.

Practical example: In Murcia (Spain), hot region during summer with temperatures exceeding 40ºC, we recommended a set of 4 fans connected together, spanning 30cm of the length of a 70cm aquarium. When connected to a timer and operated for 18-20 hours a day with occasional 30-minute breaks, mostly at night, this setup achieved a temperature drop of up to 4ºC, reducing it from 32ºC to 28-29ºC. **This fan setup cost approximately 15 euros on AliExpress.**

In summer, aquarium water evaporates rapidly. With this cooling method, water evaporation occurs slightly faster. Don't forget to add water regularly.

HOW TO ADD WATER TO THE AQUARIUM WHEN IT HAS EVAPORATED?

The water we add should be MINERAL-FREE WATER (with the lowest possible ppm), preferably distilled (though not necessary). **Very low mineralized or osmosis water works too**. **WHY?** When aquarium water evaporates, all dissolved substances remain in it; they don't evaporate. Consequently, concentrations of GH and other substances steadily increase.

9.5 WATER PARAMETERS: DISSOLVED OXYGEN AND DISSOLVED CARBON DIOXIDE

If you've read the first part of this book, you'll recall our recommendation to consider that tall, narrow aquariums offer a smaller water surface area than short, wide tanks when choosing an aquarium. We explained that **the water surface is where gas exchange occurs**: oxygen (O_2) enters the water, and carbon dioxide (CO_2) escapes. Whether your tank has a larger or smaller exposed water surface, you may need additional equipment to ensure your ecosystem receives enough oxygen.

A lack of oxygen can lead to fish asphyxiation, which if intense or prolonged, could cause diseases or even death. An excess of CO_2 (especially in CO_2-planted aquariums) can also induce acidosis in fish, causing drowsiness and a sense of suffocation. In both cases, fish might appear to "gasp" at the surface, potentially leading them to try escaping the tank by jumping out of the water.

Intoxications, such as an excessive amount of nitrates or ammonium, can also cause fish to gasp at the surface or increase their respiratory rate.

FACTORS THAT DECREASE O2 AND/OR INCREASE CO2 IN YOUR AQUARIUM

- **Smaller exchange surface** in narrow and high aquariums.
- In summer and with **high water temperatures**, the dissolved O_2 in the water decreases.
- **Presence of a "biofilm" layer on the surface** of the aquarium (sometimes a thin, whitish "web" of proteins and bacteria forms on the water's surface, making gas exchange difficult). This is caused by an excess of food and organic matter in the aquarium.
- **Excessive administration of CO2** in planted aquariums.

- **Static water surface** (increases "water surface tension," a physical property of water that hinders gas exchange).
- **Overpopulation of animals** in the aquarium, increasing O2 consumption and CO2 production.

It was once believed that having a large number of plants could also decrease O2 levels in the water since they would consume O2 at night. However, this is a misconception.

Now that we've identified the possible causes, let's explore the solutions.

HOW TO IMPROVE GAS EXCHANGE AND DISSOLVED OXYGEN IN WATER?

- **Lower the water temperature** in summer using fans.
- Use a **"Venturi effect"** filter water outlet "flute" (incorporates air by utilizing water movement).
- **Elevate the filter outlet** to the height of the aquarium surface. This will "agitate" the water, decreasing surface tension and increasing the exchange surface area. Be cautious as droplets may splash out of the aquarium, and the sound of water movement might be bothersome to some individuals.

- **To remove the biofilm layer**, use an inlet pipe with a "surface skimmer."

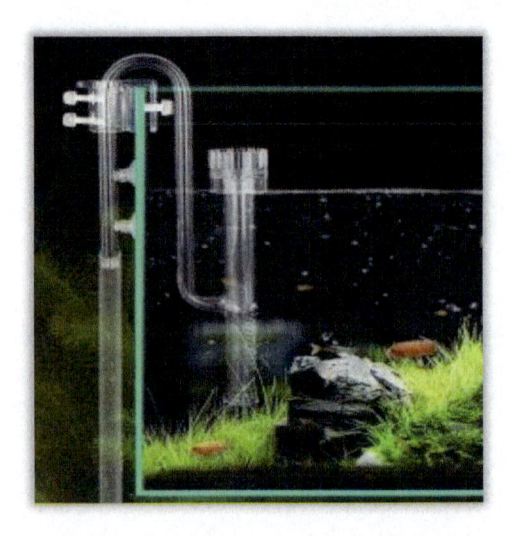

- **If you're going to administer CO2, do it in moderation,** ensuring plants can consume it adequately.

- Look for internal filters with a water outlet featuring the Venturi effect, drawing air from the surface and mixing it with the water.

- **Invest in an air pump or aerator.** A bubble pump is the most effective solution for this problem. Consider its use as a preventive measure, using bubbles as a decorative element. Oxygen deficiency is a prevalent issue, and by the time symptoms appear, a significant deficit is likely present.

In heavily planted aquariums, problems may arise primarily at night. During the day, plants oxygenate the water, but oxygen deficiency may manifest during the night. You may find fish gasping at the surface in the morning. The ultimate solution is to purchase an **air pump (with a timer, turning it on during the hours the light is off).**

The primary function of an aerator is to ensure adequate exchange of oxygen and carbon dioxide from the water to the air.

Each air bubble entering the aquarium exchanges gases with the water across the entire bubble surface, **significantly increasing the exchange surface area.**

Additionally, aerators usually include a "diffuser" (the gray-black object in the image) that increases the number of bubbles and reduces their size, further enhancing the exchange (with the same volume of air, we increase the exchange surface).

We recommend selecting an aerator that suits your preferences. One that is discreet and effective is the **"Itian aquarium air pump"** (shown in the picture). However, you can choose any other. If your aquarium is larger than 200 liters, this air pump may not be sufficient.

Great!

We've just covered the direct interventions we can make on our water to improve its quality: GH, pH, temperature, oxygenation...

Next, we'll discuss other indirect interventions (filter, filter material, aquarium cleaning and maintenance, appropriate species selection, etc.) to manage and eliminate toxic substances such as ammonia, nitrites, and nitrates.

We've already discussed some of this in chapters on "Filtration": 3, 4, and 5. In those chapters, we emphasized the significance of the filter and filter material. Now you'll understand why.

9.6 WATER PARAMETERS: AMMONIUM, NITRITES, NITRATES AND OTHER TOXICS

In addition to considering GH, KH, and pH parameters, we must be mindful of substances that can adversely affect water quality and pose a threat to aquatic life. Before introducing any products into the aquarium, ensure they are non-toxic to fish, invertebrates, plants, and the crucial bacteria that maintain our ecosystem's balance. **The only essential product to add to the water before placing it in the aquarium is a water conditioner. Under ideal conditions, there's no need to add anything else.**

Fertilizers used by some aquarists for plants can also be toxic if overdosed. For instance, in a planted aquarium, micronutrient fertilizers containing metals like copper, if overdosed, can be harmful, especially to invertebrates like shrimp.

Another product that may be justified for occasional use is aquarium bacteria.

Now, let's delve into the topic of this section!

We will discuss the toxins that every aquarist needs to understand and manage. **These toxins emphasize the importance of our filter and filtering materials: the nitrogenous compounds—ammonium, ammonia, nitrites, and nitrates.**

WHAT IS THE NITROGEN CYCLE?

The nitrogen cycle is a chemical **process facilitated by nitrifying bacteria**, transforming the **highly toxic ammonia/ammonium** in the aquarium into nitrites **(toxic),** and then nitrites into nitrates **(less toxic).**

Ammonia and ammonium promote algae growth and are highly toxic to all animals in our aquarium. However, **they pose no harm to plants**, allowing us to introduce them from the aquarium's initial setup. Ammonia **stems from** the decomposition of fish food remains, fish excrement, dead plant leaves, deceased fish, and all **other decomposing organic matter in our aquarium.**

Nitrites are an intermediate stage in the cycle and are toxic to animals while also encouraging algae growth.

Nitrates, the end product of the nitrogen cycle, will either be **consumed by plants** or algae, or **removed from the water through water changes.** In high concentrations, nitrates can also become toxic to animals. They are **well assimilated by plants** and can promote the appearance of algae, but to a much lesser extent than ammonia and nitrites.

SCHEME OF THE NITROGEN CYCLE:

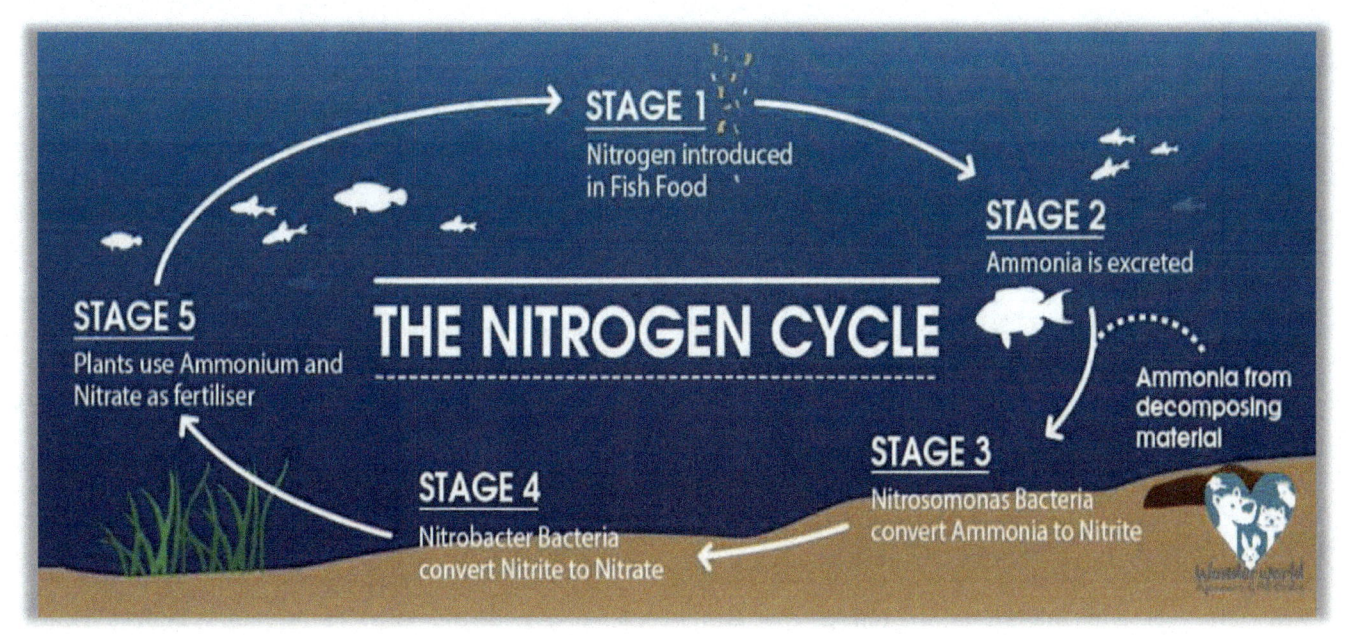

"Scheme of the nitrogen cycle"

Nitrates, the end product of the nitrogen cycle, will either be consumed by plants or algae, or removed from the water through water changes.

In our discussion of filter media, we previously mentioned chemical filter media. Activated carbon and various chemical filtration methods can effectively eliminate these nitrates, among other substances. They can be employed in aquariums without plants, reducing the risk of algae growth and the frequency of water changes. However, their use entails other considerations, outlined in Annex 1. In Chapter 10, focusing on aquarium maintenance, we will provide tips to reduce the frequency of water changes.

For the nitrogen cycle to transpire in our aquariums, we need colonies of nitrifying bacteria. The quantity of these colonies should correspond to the ammonium production in our aquarium. This ensures quick metabolization without accumulation. The more animals and food present in the aquarium, the more ammonium and ammonia there will be to "feed" the **bacteria, gradually increasing their population.**

It's crucial to understand that the increase in bacteria occurs progressively (up to the limit set by our filtration equipment) as ammonium levels in the water rise. As we'll discuss later, after completing the "cycling" process, we cannot introduce the entire animal population into our ecosystem at once. It must be a gradual process over several weeks. <u>Why?</u> **Because the bacteria in the ecosystem must grow progressively and in sync with the animal population's growth.**

The significance of our filtration equipment lies in the distribution of nitrifying bacteria throughout the aquarium, substrate, plants, and the water column. However, **the primary concentration and reproduction of bacterial colonies occur in the pores of the filter material.** Thus, the **maximum number of colonies and the highest rate of ammonium and nitrites transformation in your ecosystem mainly depend on:**

- Filter flow rate.
- Filter´s filter material capacity.
- **Quantity and quality of biological filter material in the filter.**

WHAT IS AQUARIUM CYCLING?

Now that you understand what the nitrogen cycle is, let's delve into aquarium cycling. **Aquarium cycling involves triggering the nitrogen cycle in our aquarium** in proportion to ammonium and nitrite production.

Your primary task is to <u>wait</u> until your aquarium, especially the filter, is populated with bacteria. If you've just acquired an aquarium, waiting a month before adding fish is not what you'd prefer. However, this waiting period allows you to carefully select plants (if applicable) and fish for your aquarium or refine certain project details.

GENERAL INFORMATION ON CYCLING

1. **Most of the process is automatic. Patience is key**, along with small daily feedings to the aquarium.
2. **The process can be expedited** to last 2 to 3 weeks and even be ready **in less than 1 week.**
3. Keep in mind that placing fish, shrimp, or any other animals **in the uncycled aquarium renders the water toxic**. The probability of most or nearly all animals dying is very high. In the best case, they may survive with significant physiological stress. Fish species sensitive to these toxins or invertebrates like "neocarid shrimp" are unlikely to survive in such conditions.
4. Other guides may suggest using various tests for cycling control:
    a. Nitrite test.
    b. b. Nitrate test.
    c. Ammonium test.

    We believe it's a significant expense and unnecessary. If you opt to use any, we recommend the nitrate test (NO3). **Once nitrates appear in the aquarium, the cycling is complete.** You can then use it to measure the nitrate levels in the aquarium.

5. **If you can afford it,** we suggest using 2 products. If you can only choose one, opt for bacteria.
    a. **Utilize bacteria to initiate the aquarium's cycle.** This ensures the aquarium is cycled in 3-4 weeks without requiring a test (<u>it could be cycled in less than 1 week</u>).
    b. **Use a nitrate (NO3) test.** It helps monitor the water **and confirm the cycling is complete**. Later, if issues arise with the aquarium, you can use it to check the nitrate level. In a cycled aquarium, the ammonium and nitrite levels should be 0, eliminating the need to monitor them.

The other extreme is to proceed blindly, without conducting any tests or using bacteria, and monitor the process for 45 days. However, this isn't the most advisable approach due to the risk that the aquarium may remain uncycled even after the full period.

HOW TO CYCLE?

Cycling commences with the presence of ammonia or ammonium in the water. As days pass, colonies of nitrifying bacteria naturally establish and multiply, gradually reducing ammonia and nitrite levels to 0 after 30 to 45 days. **There are two ways to initiate cycling (introducing ammonia into the water): using fish flake food** (which decomposes to produce ammonia) **or directly adding ammonia.**

Adding ammonia directly has its advantages, notably that it does not increase phosphates in the aquarium (which facilitates algae growth). However, a major drawback is the need to purchase an ammonia test. We initially included this method in the guide but later removed it, considering other options more effective and economical, both in terms of speed and efficiency.

Plants can be introduced right from the start of the cycle without any issues.

A. HOW TO CYCLE THE AQUARIUM WITH FISH FOOD?

Assuming everything is set up:

- The aquarium is filled with substrate at the bottom.
- The filter and heater (if using one) have been running for 24 hours.
- Decoration can be added during or after the cycling process.
- Natural plants can be added before, during, or after cycling, as preferred.
- Once plants are added, you can set the light on a timer for cycles of 7-9 hours. If you're not adding plants, we'll discuss when to turn on the light later.

Steps to follow:

1. On the day you fill the aquarium, **start adding fish food** to the water—2-3 flakes (or an equivalent amount of another type of fish food) every 24 hours per 100L (4-5 flakes for more than 200L). Follow this ratio if your aquarium has a greater volume. **Continue adding flakes until around day 21**. Do not exceed the recommended amount, as it may prolong the cycling time instead of shortening it.
2. After 30 days, start testing for nitrates. As soon as they start to rise, the aquarium is cycled.

If you decide to add bacteria to the water (we'll discuss how shortly), you can use a test after 7-10 days. However, bear in mind that the colonies may not be large enough to start introducing fish at this point.

E. NATURAL CYCLING EVOLUTION GRAPH

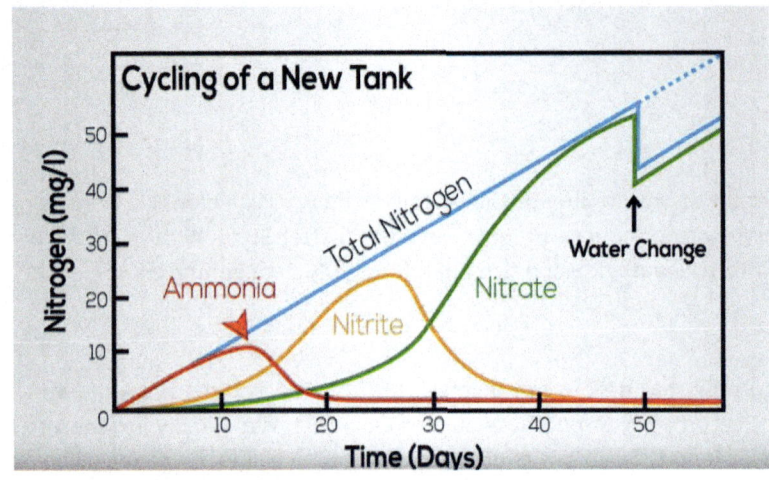

Cycling of a New Tank

Around **21 days**, nitrite concentration in the water surpasses 0. Nitrate concentration can be equal to or greater than 0. **This marks the time to stop adding flakes** to the aquarium.

After cycling, regular testing is unnecessary (unless you have high-maintenance plants), but it can be beneficial if issues arise.

"Natural cycling (without bacteria or other methods)"

Remember: Some individuals use fish to cycle aquariums, but this subjects the fish to immense stress, choking sensation, potential illness, and eventual death. There are better and quicker methods.

F. THE VALUES OF A CYCLED AQUARIUM

- **Ammonia** level: 0
- **Nitrite** level: 0
- **Nitrate** level: equal to or greater than 0

G. WHAT TO DO IF NITRATES REMAIN 0 AFTER 30 DAYS?

If you haven't added bacteria to the aquarium, it's possible that cycling is not complete. **We recommend obtaining the bacteria** and starting to use them following the manufacturer's instructions. Treat this as the first day of cycling.

If you've already added bacteria to the aquarium (the ones we'll recommend or another reliable brand), and you've done so according to the manufacturer's instructions, **and 14-21 days have passed** while following the other steps we've outlined, **it's highly likely that your aquarium is cycled.** Any issue might stem from a problem with the test's usage. **In this case,** proceed with weekly water changes and continue adding bacteria according to the manufacturer's instructions. **After 4 weeks, begin introducing animals.**

HOW TO ACCELERATE AQUARIUM CYCLING?

When aiming to speed up aquarium cycling, we have two options: purchasing cycling bacteria or obtaining gravel or biological filter material from an already cycled and stable aquarium.

A. CYCLING THE AQUARIUM BY ADDING BACTERIAL PREPARATIONS

Experience has shown us that the bacteria in these preparations do NOT substitute for the natural cycling process that typically takes 30 to 45 days, but they can be an effective method to ensure that our aquarium is fully cycled and ready for the initial animal inhabitants after 4 weeks.

However, the downside is the cost of these products. We've tried several and would recommend two products that have yielded good results:

Azoo plus Ultrabioguard

Microbe-Lift Special Blend

In our experience, following the manufacturer's instructions, the ammonium and nitrite levels after 7 to 10 days were consistently at 0, indicating that **the aquarium could be cycled in less than a week.** It's crucial to note that just because the cycle is complete, it doesn't mean the aquarium is immediately ready for fish. The bacteria need time to multiply, and abrupt changes in the amount of decomposing matter could destabilize the aquarium and elevate ammonium concentrations.

B. HOW TO COMBINE THE FLAKING METHOD WITH BACTERIA?

Begin by adding 2-3 flakes per 100 liters every day from the first day of filling the aquarium. Four days after filling, add the initial dose of bacteria following the manufacturer's instructions. Continue adding flakes until day 14. If you have the tests, you can conduct the first test after 14 days. Most likely, the nitrate levels will be > 0 in the water. Although the aquarium is cycled, the bacterial population is still small, so we recommend allowing it to develop for at least until week 4 (2 weeks after you stop adding flakes). **If you're eager to introduce the first fish, you can do so in the first week, but ensure a gradual introduction.**

After 14 days, perform the first water change of 20-25%, and continue with weekly changes (approximately 20-30%). After 28 days, **start introducing the first fish and progressively add fish every 2 weeks. Avoid adding too many fish at once,** as a surge in decomposing organic matter can overwhelm the bacteria's capacity to process all the ammonium, resulting in a potentially toxic increase of ammonium in the aquarium. Further details on introducing the first fish will be discussed later in this section.

In Chapter 14: "The Inhabitants of the Aquarium," we will cover selecting species and determining the recommended maximum number of fish for your ecosystem.

We suggest utilizing the day of the water change to introduce new fish into the aquarium. You can administer the maintenance doses of bacteria recommended by the manufacturer upon arrival (optional). While it's not necessary to add bacteria to the aquarium at every water change, it may be beneficial to do so upon introducing new animals to the aquarium or after cleaning the filter, for instance.

Conclusion regarding the use of bacteria: Bacteria are **not essential** for the cycling or maintenance of an aquarium, and they are relatively expensive. **However**, if you choose to invest in them, **they will ensure a well-cycled aquarium after 30 days**. Beyond this initial cycling, you can continue to add them periodically when introducing new fish, after cleaning the filter, or in case of issues related to an excess of organic matter.

Any claims suggesting that you can cycle an aquarium and immediately introduce fish 2 days after filling the aquarium with certain cycling bacteria are either incorrect or omitting vital information. It takes longer for them to multiply on your filter media. **If you start introducing fish within the first few days, do it gradually and not all at once.**

C. HOW TO CYCLE AN AQUARIUM WITH FILTER MEDIA FROM A CYCLED AQUARIUM?

This is the fastest method. The aquarium is effectively cycled from the moment you introduce "cycled" biological material from another of your aquariums or from another partner's aquarium. If you have a sufficient amount of "cycled" biological material, you could start introducing animals (always progressively) from the first or second day. **We will cover how to introduce fish to the aquarium in the next section.**

The layer of filter media where the nitrifying bacteria colonies reside is the biological media layer. If you obtain approximately a third or more of the total filter media needed (as per our recommendations), you could introduce some animals from day one.

If the quantity is smaller, it will expedite the cycling, but it would be too risky to introduce fish so soon. In such cases, follow the steps outlined in the previous section: how to combine the flake method with bacteria, but refrain from adding more bacteria.

If you are very eager to cycle your aquarium, you can consider purchasing cycled biologic material or borrowing them from local Facebook or WhatsApp groups in your area.

There are also bacteria in the water, especially in the substrate, allowing for other approaches:

- Mix substrate from an already cycled aquarium with new substrate. Adding at least 10-20% of the total substrate will expedite the cycling, and you could start adding fish after 4 weeks, following the steps in the previous section: how to combine the flake method with bacteria, but without adding more bacteria.
- Combine the new substrate with unwashed river sand and its original mud (this is the best way to introduce pathogenic microorganisms to our aquariums, **so we strongly advise against this**).

HOW TO INTRODUCE THE FIRST FISH INTO THE AQUARIUM?

Once the cycling is complete, utilize the last water change to introduce the first fish to the aquarium. Starting with 2-3 small fish (less than 5 cm) or 1-2 larger fish per 50 liters would be an appropriate amount to begin with. These figures are approximate.

If you have bacteria, administer the "maintenance dose" recommended by the manufacturer 24 hours after placing the fish in the water. Every 14 days, after water changes, you can repeat this procedure to add fish until you reach the total number of fish you can and/or want to keep in your aquarium.

Just as we discuss fish, the same applies to shrimp or other animals. Always introduce them gradually, considering the figures provided to gauge the amount of new inhabitants your aquarium can handle.

RECOMMENDATIONS TO CONSIDER DURING CYCLING

If you opt not to use a test, which is an option, and haven't found a partner who can provide filter material, we recommend utilizing the saved funds to purchase aquarium bacteria. Following the advice of cycling with flakes + bacteria, your aquarium will be fully cycled in 1 month. We can divide the cycling into 2 phases. **The initial phase** begins when the aquarium is just filled, there's ammonium present but no bacteria yet, **and NO nitrites**. **The second phase** starts when the first nitrifying bacteria are established, and **nitrites begin to rise**.

If you do a cycling with flakes and without adding bacteria, the first phase will last approximately 21 days. **If you have added bacteria, dividing this advice into two parts is NOT necessary** and can be understood as general recommendations. With bacteria, the second phase of cycling would start at 5-7 days or less.

During the two phases of aquarium cycling, here are our recommendations:

1ST PHASE. Before nitrite levels rise:

- Do not turn on the lighting, unless you have decided to plant from day one. Nitrifying bacteria colonies proliferate better without light.
- Some guides suggest not adding plants during this phase. However, based on our experience, this does not delay cycling. Additionally, starting with small-sized or a small quantity of plants, it's not likely to pose a problem for cycling.
- Do not turn off the filter (the filter should always remain on) or clean it. During the aquarium cycling, bacteria settle in the filter, so cleaning it will likely slowdown that process.
- Do not use activated carbon or any other chemical filter media that removes ammonium or nitrites.
- Ensure good aeration of the water. Nitrifying bacteria are aerobic and grow best in well-oxygenated conditions. We discussed how to aerate the aquarium effectively in the previous section.
- Maintain a temperature of 24 to 26°C, which is optimal for the proliferation of nitrifying bacteria. If it's a cold-water aquarium and it's winter, purchasing a heater is not necessary. The process will be slower, but the aquarium will still cycle.

2ND PHASE. Nitrites begin to rise (approximately 21 days); there are already bacteria that transform ammonia into nitrites:

- Do not add more flake food. The flakes you're adding today take 10-14 days to decompose, so you will continue to increase the bacteria population for at least 14-21 days after you stop adding them (the time it will take for the first fish to arrive).
- If you had planned to include some natural plants in your aquarium and haven't done so yet, this could be a good time. They help eliminate the remaining ammonia/ammonium and assist the second group of bacteria in transforming nitrites into nitrates, thereby beginning the reduction of nitrates.
- If you haven't done so already, turn on the lighting, even if you don't have fish or plants. Our ecosystem requires alternating periods of light and dark. The optimal photoperiod for aquarium plants is at least 7-10 hours per day (for tropical fish and plant aquariums, 12-14 hours may be suitable, although keep in mind that in nature at dawn

and dusk, the light is not as intense). If you don't have plants, a similar light cycle of 7-9 hours, although with lower light intensity, would be adequate.
- Perform the first water change. Begin weekly water changes of 20-30% of the aquarium water (initially recommended, but as we will discuss later, with a good population of healthy natural plants, water changes are hardly necessary).

WHAT TO DO WHEN THE CYCLING IS OVER?

With the **nitrate** test, you can monitor the nitrate levels of the aquarium. Ideally, **they should be around 10 mg/l if you have plants and as close to 0 mg/liter if you do not**. We recommend that they should **always be below 30 mg/l. If you have neocaridine shrimp, it's better to keep them below 20 mg/l**. In any case, if you have followed the steps we've outlined, you can start introducing your fish without conducting any tests.

9.7 WATER: LATEST TIPS

In addition to considering GH, KH, and pH parameters, we need to be mindful of substances that can detrimentally affect water quality and prove toxic to aquatic organisms.

Tap water can also contain varying concentrations of zinc and copper. It's important to note that these metals might exist in drinking water at levels that **can be toxic to our fish and invertebrates**. Generally, metal toxicity is more pronounced in soft, acidic water compared to hard, alkaline water.

Certain aquarium water conditioners contain EDTA, an effective metal chelator that mitigates short-term toxicity. Plants can provide long-term protection.

MEASURES TO REDUCE METAL TOXICITY

Here's a list of measures you can implement:

- Utilize reverse **osmosis water** for water changes (keep in mind that this will result in very soft water, **necessitating potential salt additions** or mixing with tap water).
- Use **conditioners** containing metal chelators like EDTA.
- Employ peat filtration, which exchanges H+ (acidifying the water) for metal ions (added complexity).
- Increase water hardness, as calcium shields organisms from metals.
- **Maintain a planted aquarium**, promoting proper plant growth, and prune as needed to manage excess.
- Allow humic substances from the decomposition of deceased plants to accumulate.

Actions that can escalate metal toxicity include:

- **Water changes,** which remove humic acids. If tap water is contaminated with metals, each change might introduce more.
- **Fertilize the plants.**

- **Utilizing surface skimming and activated carbon,** which also eliminate these decomposed substances from plants.

You're already familiar with all the necessary parameters!

Managing these parameters adequately ensures a completely healthy and balanced ecosystem. *These parameters will serve as the foundation for all your future projects.*

In the future, you may encounter the need to manage new parameters, such as plant nutrients (nitrates, phosphates, potassium, etc.), advanced knowledge about GH/KH salts for highly specific fish or invertebrate species, filtration materials with specific properties, and more.

With the knowledge you've just acquired, everything will be significantly easier for you.

10 AQUARIUM AUTOMATION, MAINTENANCE AND CARE

Before delving into the main topic of this section (which covers aquarium maintenance), we want to emphasize the importance of automating routine processes in the aquarium. There's no need to spend time manually turning the lamp or air pump on and off. We can also automate the feeding process using automatic feeders. Apart from reducing worry, automation benefits the aquarium ecosystem by establishing routines for plants and animals, ultimately enhancing their stability.

10.1 USE TIMERS: AUTOMATE WHAT CAN BE AUTOMATED

Timers help establish schedules for our aquarium, ensuring that fish and plants, like other living beings, have routines involving periods of rest and activity. **Additionally, timers never forget.**

1. Utilize **a light timer:** It's crucial to have a light timer. LED lamps that include timers are available, or you can purchase one separately. We recommend 7-10 hours of light per day. If you can adjust light intensity to mimic sunrise and sunset, you can extend the duration. Keep in mind that tropical fish and plants typically experience 12-14 hours of light in their natural habitat. If you don't have plants, reduce the light intensity, but maintain lighting for 7-9 hours.
2. In summer, **if you have a fan to cool** the aquarium, connect it to a timer to adjust the operating hours based on water temperature (as explained in the temperature management chapter: 9.3).
3. **If you have an air pump**, you can run it 24 hours a day or connect it to a timer based on your requirements. For example, if you have plants, you can connect it at night since they do not produce oxygen during this time. If your goal is to oxygenate the water, you can plug and unplug it in 30-minute intervals.
4. **Utilize timers for any programmable actions.**
5. For vacations or daily use, **automatic feeders** are very useful. Ensure you select one that provides accurate dosing of food. We've had positive experiences with "Autofood" from JBL.

Remember: The filter and heater must ALWAYS remain on.

Both digital and analog timers are available. Generally, analog timers are more affordable, easy to use, and highly durable. There are many options to choose from—pick the most cost-effective or the one that suits your preferences. As always, AliExpress offers budget-friendly options if you're willing to wait. Amazon provides a good price-to-convenience ratio. You can find these timers in nearly any store, both online and local.

111

DON'T FORGET THE POWER STRIP WITH AN EXTENSION CORD AND MULTIPLE PLUGS. Do not purchase one with fewer than 6 plugs, unless you intend to buy more than one.

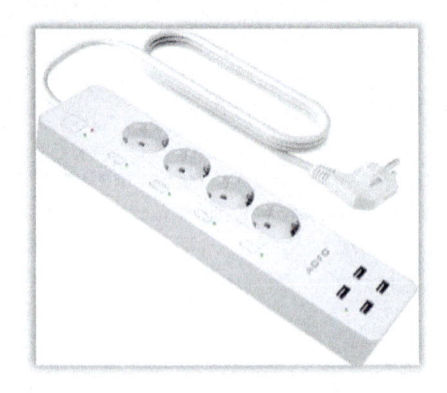

We also want to introduce you to power strips with multiple sockets and wifi controllers. You can program the schedules using your cell phone, and they occupy less space.

In this scenario, timers are no longer necessary.

You can find them for around 20 euros on AliExpress. At this price point, it's a compelling option, especially considering the cost is comparable to buying a power strip with several timers separately. It might also be more convenient than manually adjusting schedules.

A significant drawback is that some of these devices may reset if there's a power outage in your house, disconnecting everything even when power is restored. It's advisable to connect the filter and heater separately to a standard socket or power strip, or ensure this doesn't occur in your situation.

10.2 DAILY AQUARIUM CARE

1. **Turning the lights on and off:** The aquarium light should be on for 7-9 hours, and the on/off cycle should be consistent every day.

2. **Check the temperature:** Nowadays, with the availability of heaters in the market, maintaining the temperature within the ideal range is straightforward. Your task is to occasionally check the temperature, every day or every few days, using a thermometer to ensure the heater is functioning correctly and connected.

3. **Summer:** As summer approaches, you'll notice that the temperature (depending on your region) falls within the ideal range without the heater. You can disconnect it and remove it from the aquarium until the next winter. When the temperature exceeds 28°C, it's time to install and run the fan (in most ecosystems).

4. **Ensure the filters and air pump are operational:** Prolonged filter malfunction can destabilize the aquarium. Toxins will accumulate over time, negatively affecting water quality and your fish's health. Moreover, nitrifying bacteria require oxygen to thrive, so if the flow is halted for an extended period, they could be adversely affected (to date, we haven't encountered issues with stagnant water for 2 or 3 days). A heavily planted aquarium can almost completely substitute the filter's function, preventing problems even if the filter stops working altogether.

5. **Feed the fish 2-3 times a day:** Offer small amounts of food. If you observe that your fish quickly consume the food and continue to eat, you can provide a little more.

It's important to dispel the misconception that fish should be fed only once a day or every few days. Tropical fish do NOT eat unnecessarily. If you've overfed them, they won't consume the excess food, resulting in accumulated leftovers. On the other hand, cold-water fish like goldfish, following their seasonal cycle in nature, eat substantially during warm months.

In addition to dry food, you can offer live and frozen food such as artemia, daphnia, red mosquito larvae, etc., which are available at pet stores. Alternatively, you can rear them yourself.

Clear signs of overfeeding include: cloudy water, foul-smelling water, and leftover food settling at the bottom the next day.

10.3 WEEKLY AQUARIUM CARE

1. **Vacuuming the Aquarium:** You can utilize the water change to siphon off remnants of decomposing organic matter from the bottom of the aquarium. For planted aquariums (with roots in the substrate), this may not be necessary as plants can utilize decomposing matter to nourish themselves and oxygenate the substrate through their roots.

2. **Water Changes:** To remove nitrates and replenish consumed substances, it's generally ideal to perform weekly partial water changes, amounting to 20-30% of the total aquarium water. It's possible to maintain planted aquariums without water changes for months, as plants filter out waste for nourishment and growth. We will discuss this further when we delve into plants.

3. **Refilling Evaporated Water**: When adding water to the aquarium due to evaporation, ensure it is MINERAL-FREE WATER (or has minimal minerals in parts per million). Ideally, distilled water is suitable (though not necessary), but weakly mineralized or osmosis water will also suffice. WHY? When aquarium water evaporates, dissolved substances do not evaporate. Consequently, the concentrations of GH and other dissolved substances in the water gradually increase. IMPORTANT: If you opt for distilled water, ensure it's free of additives.

4. **Algae Removal from Glass (Aesthetic Reason):** Various instruments like magnets or scrapers are available to remove algae from the glass. In the end, the simplest and most effective method (for smaller aquariums) is to use a credit card or a similar object as a scraper. Removing algae is primarily aesthetic; they aren't harmful to the aquarium. On the contrary, they assist in reducing toxins. If they appear in large quantities and suddenly, it's a good indicator that something is amiss. In well-planted aquariums with a good substrate, this problem may never arise.

10.4 OTHER CARE

Case-Specific:

1. **Prefilter Replacement:** Every 3-7 days, depending on the decline in filter output flow. **If you have a metal grid prefilter, it's likely that the cleaning intervals will be much longer.**
2. **Filter Cleaning: ALWAYS** use aquarium water for cleaning. The cleaning frequency varies greatly from one aquarium to another, depending on factors such as filter type, size, fish quantity, presence of plants, and more. We'll delve into this further below, but cleaning intervals can range from weeks to years depending on each case.
3. **Bacteria Addition (if present):** If feasible, follow the manufacturer's instructions and add bacteria at each water change to promote stability in your aquarium water. However, they are NOT essential.

   Situations where bacteria could be beneficial:

- When introducing a large number of fish to the aquarium within a short period.
- Sudden increase in organic matter decomposition, exceeding the levels that our filtration can handle: overpopulation, overfeeding.
- Accidental reduction in filter bacteria population due to filter cleaning errors.

Care for Planted Aquariums:

1. **Removing unsightly or fallen leaves:** For aesthetic reasons. Dead leaves also constitute decomposing matter that can nourish the plants.

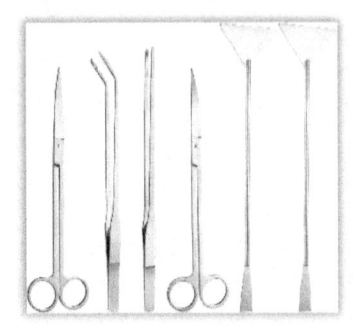

   We recommend against unnecessary spending on a pruning kit. There are options, like the one shown in this image, made of stainless steel, of high quality, and priced between 12-17 euros on AliExpress.

2. **Changing Fluorescent Tubes (for planted aquariums):** Tubes should be changed every 9-12 months (for planted aquariums with high plant requirements). Even if they are functional, the quality and intensity of light diminish after this time. If the aquarium has more than one tube, it's advisable to change one initially and then the other later, preventing a sudden change in light intensity.

   If you have LED lights, these changes can occur every 2-4 years or more.

3. **Fertilization:** This varies considerably based on factors such as the type of nutrients being used, testing frequency, weekly or daily fertilization, and more. If you've used a nutrient-rich substrate from a store or have made your own with terrestrial plant substrate, this may not be necessary. In upcoming chapters, we'll provide tips and video links useful for starting a planted aquarium.

4. **Pruning:** To create space and allow plants to continue growing, consuming toxic substances in the water.

Remember: Significant, abrupt changes in the aquarium can disrupt the ecosystem balance achieved during the cycling and maturation period.

If you only intend to change the decoration, you can temporarily relocate the fish to a holding tank with the filter running, set up the new arrangement, and reintroduce the fish and plants. A minor imbalance likely won't cause significant issues. If you have a "bacteria canister" on hand, you can use it to repopulate some of the lost bacteria

10.5 WATER CHANGES

The primary purpose of water changes is to remove toxic substances that can only be eliminated through this method, with specialized filter materials or by employing plants. **The critical toxicant necessitating regular water changes is nitrate.** If you have plants, water changes become valuable for micronutrient replenishment if a nutrient substrate is unavailable.

In addition to water changes, it's advisable to trim unhealthy leaves and siphon the substrate to reduce decomposing organic matter. Implementing these tasks systematically will prevent numerous problems in the future. However, in heavily planted aquariums with many plants rooted in the substrate, such cleaning may be unnecessary.

In some regions and during certain times of the year, tap water may have high nitrate concentrations. To address this, using bottled water or partially treated osmosis water for water changes is sufficient. Plants or chemical filtration can also be employed.

HOW ARE THEY MADE?

Approximately 3 weeks after initiating the cycling process, or 14 days (if bacteria were used), conduct the first water change. Remove 20-30% of the aquarium water and replace it with dechlorinated new water adjusted to your desired ppm levels (as explained in the chapter on water parameters: 9.2). Additionally, keep the following in mind:

- Prepare the water in advance in bottles or containers a few hours or even days earlier (at least 10-15 minutes), and add the conditioner (we recommend Seachem's PRIME). After completing the water change, you can refill the bottles, add the water conditioner, and have them ready for the following week.

- REMEMBER: **The TDS meter doesn't help approximate the GH of water in our aquarium;** it only estimates the GH of the water before adding it to the aquarium. In other words, if the water you add during changes measures 150 ppm, the GH will be around 8. However, if your aquarium's ppm is 150, the GH won't be 8; it will be lower due to other dissolved particles, such as nitrates. If you insist that your aquarium water reads 150 ppm, the GH will likely range between 2 and 5.

- Add conditioned water adjusted to the appropriate ppm for the species in your aquarium.

During summer, when refilling evaporated water from the aquarium with osmosis water or very low hardness bottled water, the hardness in your aquarium may gradually increase. Don't worry; if you maintain your weekly water change routine, this change won't be significant. When water evaporates, dissolved molecules remain in the water.

HOW OFTEN SHOULD WATER CHANGES BE DONE?

The frequency of water changes is highly specific to each aquarium, influenced by numerous factors. Eventually, you'll become an expert on your aquarium and better understand how often you need to perform water changes. Until then, we'll provide guidelines to give you a rough idea and help you adjust the frequency of water changes.

FACTORS DECREASING THE FREQUENCY OF WATER CHANGES

Noticeably, factors reducing water change frequency are the same factors that reduce nitrate levels in the water, either before or after their formation.

A. GENERAL RECOMMENDATIONS

- **Planted Aquariums:** Plants reduce nitrates and many other toxic substances in the water. Heavily planted aquariums with healthy plant growth can reduce the need for water changes to once every few weeks or even months. However, it's important to note that water changes also serve as a way to provide micronutrients to our plants. If you have a completely inert substrate, you'll likely need to perform these changes.
- **Few Animals and Fish:** The fewer the fish, the less food, fewer excreta, and longer intervals between water changes due to lower nitrate accumulation.
- **Organic Matter Removal:** Pruning, removing dead leaves, deceased animals, siphoning the aquarium during water changes, etc., result in less decomposing organic matter and subsequently lower nitrate levels.
- **Avoid Overfeeding:** Not overfeeding the animals in the aquarium is essential.
- **Proper Use of Chemical Filtration or Specific Filter Materials:** In Annex 1, we'll explain how to use them. While not essential, they can make maintenance a bit easier. These techniques are primarily meant for aquariums without plants.

A. BASSED ON AQUARIUM TYPE

- **Plant-Free Aquariums**: For such setups, weekly changes are necessary, primarily to remove nitrates from the water.
- **Aquariums with Plants:** In heavily planted aquariums, especially those with a nutrient-rich substrate (either specific for planted aquariums or homemade substrate), the intervals between water changes can be extended to 2-3 weeks or longer. Although not recommended, these changes correct errors in micronutrient fertilization and address excesses or deficiencies in macronutrients, which we haven't discussed until now. Plants also release hormones into the water to compete with other plants and algae in the aquarium; water changes can help regulate these substances.
- **Aquariums with Chemical Filtration or Methods to Reduce Nitrates:** Although uncommon, if our aquarium isn't planted, we won't require nitrates or phosphates for plants. Proper use of chemical filtration can considerably extend water change intervals, up to 3 weeks or even longer. Details on this can be found in Annex 1.

10.6 HOW TO SIPHON THE AQUARIUM?

Search for a YouTube video demonstrating this process. It's quite simple, and watching a video will provide a clear understanding. The siphons demonstrated in the video are a good option, and similar ones are available inexpensively on AliExpress.

10.7 HOW OFTEN AND HOW SHOULD I CLEAN THE AQUARIUM FILTER?

The biological filter media should always be cleaned with aquarium water. The remaining filter components, including mechanical filtration, can be cleaned using tap water. Typically, filter cleaning should be performed every 2-3 months on average, but this frequency varies greatly depending on the individual case, ranging from less than a month to several years.

Determining when to clean the filter is straightforward. Most filters have water flow regulators. As the flow rate decreases, adjust it. When you've increased the flow to the maximum and it's still reduced by 30-40%, it's time to clean the filter.

If you've opted for a pre-filter in the inlet pipe, clean it every 3-7 days (when the water outflow decreases), particularly if it's a foam sponge. This filter can also be cleaned with tap water. If you use a metal or plastic grid pre-filter, it may not require cleaning for weeks or even months.

Remember, biological filter material should be replaced every 2-3 years, although it can last up to 5 or 10 years in some cases. When replacing it, do so gradually over several weeks, changing it in stages over 30-60 days.

FACTORS EXTENDING FILTER CLEANING PERIODS

- **Plant-Free Aquariums:** Plant residues won't enter the filter, maintaining its flow rate.
- **Few Fish and Other Animals:** The fewer the fish, the less food and organic debris passing through the filter.
- **Organic Matter Removal:** Pruning when needed, removing dead leaves, deceased animals, siphoning during water changes, etc.
- **Avoid Overfeeding:** Not overfeeding the animals.
- **Use of a Prefilter:** With a prefilter sponge, large organic debris is prevented from entering the filter (though you'll need to clean this sponge frequently).

Congratulations!

If you've reached this point, you've made significant progress. Some colleagues take years or never fully grasp some of the concepts explained here. You're already on your way, and this forms the foundation for all your projects.

The primary objective is now behind us, and we won't delve too deeply in the subsequent chapters. However, we still have important topics to cover, such as the inclusion or exclusion of natural plants in our aquarium. ***We'll discuss decoration, planted aquariums, and aquarium inhabitants.***

11 THE DECORATION

The project you intend to develop will significantly influence decision-making in many preceding sections, such as the choice of the tank, the filter and its appropriate sizing, the consideration of using chemical filtration or not, adjustments of water parameters based on species, and the lighting requirements, among others.

Let's explore various options and get started!

When selecting equipment for your aquarium, especially **if you don't have a specific project like a biotope in mind**, it's crucial to consider the fish species you want (size, tropical, cold or warm water, etc.). However, **the most crucial decision is whether your aquarium will host plants** and, if so, what type of plants and their requirements.

Why? If you've been paying attention, you'll realize that certain decisions hinge on whether your aquarium will host plants and the types of plants you choose. Some pivotal considerations include:

- **Tank Size:** The size of the tank is influenced by the species of fish you intend to keep. For instance, aquariums for "cichlids" or "goldfish" require a larger minimum size compared to those for "tetras" or "rasboras". Moreover, if you opt for plants with high requirements, the costs of equipment significantly increase, almost doubling when doubling the tank size.
- **Filter:** Heavily planted aquariums have a constant turnover of organic matter. Well-cared-for plants with high requirements can grow rapidly and may obstruct the filter's inlet and outlet. If you have a small filter, it will necessitate more frequent cleaning. However, in heavily planted setups, healthy plants can keep nitrate and other toxic substance levels low without relying on a large filter. In fact, very planted low-tech aquariums can sometimes function without a filter (although this isn't recommended for beginners).
- **Lighting**: If plants aren't part of your setup, minimal lighting is adequate for the fish. However, you may choose to invest a bit more in RGB LED lighting to enhance the colors of the fish. If you decide to have plants, appropriate lighting (avoiding over-lighting) is crucial for their growth. High-tech setups with plants that have high requirements will necessitate higher intensity lighting.
- **Substrate Choice:** Chapter 7, "Substrates," provides essential information for making this decision. In summary, inert gravel can be used for both planted and unplanted tanks. However, for enhanced plant development, superior substrate types are available and are recommended for plants with high requirements. Examples include JBL Manado or preparing a homemade nutrient substrate covered by a layer of inert gravel (a cost-effective option, albeit with higher risk for beginners).
- **Chemical Filtration:** While chemical filtration can save time by reducing the need for water changes, it is generally incompatible with plants.

Consider the amount of time you have available. In general, setting up and maintaining planted aquariums with low to medium requirements is more expensive than their non-planted counterparts. The costs for a high-tech planted aquarium are significantly higher and incomparable to other types of aquariums. Additionally, as the complexity of the aquarium increases, especially with high-tech planted setups, the time commitment required also increases. Keep in mind that plants aren't the only factor to consider; for instance, cichlids are generally more expensive than tropical fish.

The easiest aquarium to maintain once established is a planted one with low to medium requirements, using homemade substrate or JBL Manado with JBL AquaBasis. **Why?** Once the ecosystem stabilizes in about two months and the plants have grown sufficiently:

- **Water changes** will hardly be necessary.
- **No additional fertilizers** are required.
- **There's no need to siphon** the substrate.
- **Filter cleaning** will almost **never** be necessary.
- If you have automation as recommended (light, aerator, even an automatic feeder), **the only essential task will be pruning** the plants every 1-2 weeks to facilitate their growth and maintain water clarity.

You might already have a project in mind. If not, you can find numerous ideas on YouTube, social media, and various websites. There are plenty of videos and images where fellow enthusiasts present their projects—cold water setups, tropical water setups, with or without plants, utilizing rocks or just aquascaping. We'd like to share two contrasting examples of aquariums to provide a sense of the spectrum:

Goldfish aquarium: Approximately 240 liters in volume, a simple setup with silica sand as substrate, a quality filter, and basic lighting. It requires relatively little maintenance (weekly water changes and substrate siphoning) and doesn't necessitate much additional equipment (though chemical filtration could be added), making it relatively inexpensive.

Planted Aquarium - "Dutch Type Aquascape" Inspired: A tank of about 40-50 liters with nutrient tests, liquid fertilizers, special substrates, CO2 injection, powerful lighting, and more. This setup requires an average of at least 7-10 hours per week (from an experienced person) to keep it in perfect conditions. It demands perseverance and technical skills that need to be honed over time. Moreover, the overall cost for this project would be slightly higher than the previous example, despite having only 5 times less tank volume.

It's important to note that the total budget for setting up an aquarium roughly doubles when the water volume is doubled.

There are no inherently better or worse projects—each project is personal and the right fit for the individual. Find what you like, gather ideas, and customize it to your preferences. We'll revisit these two examples in Annex 2 at the end of the book, where we'll delve into the necessary equipment for each and provide cost breakdowns.

11.1 GENERAL TIPS FOR DECORATION

- Plan the aquarium's decoration and layout, either by jotting down notes or creating a simple **outline or sketch** to avoid overlooking any aspect.
- If you already have the materials, **create the composition outside the tank** and perform necessary tests to avoid causing damage to the aquarium glass. **Capture a photograph of the setup for reference.**
- Keep in mind the natural tendencies of various **fish species**, ensuring there are ample **hiding spots or resting areas** in your chosen decor.
- Tailor the space in the aquarium based on the species you plan to house, **leaving some areas free** and undecorated as needed for each project.
- When incorporating plants, arrange them by species, **positioning taller, leafier ones towards the back.** This creates different visual planes, adds depth, and helps conceal equipment such as pipes and wiring.
- **Avoid placing objects** in the tank that **haven't been specifically manufactured or prepared for aquarium use**, especially plastic, ceramic, wood, rocks, or glass.
- Exercise **caution with sharp objects** to prevent harm to the fish.
- Avoid objects that can rust, as rust is toxic.
- If using wood or rocks you've collected yourself, consult specific guides to determine suitability and prepare them accordingly. Certain woods and rocks may harbor harmful microorganisms.
- The same caution applies to rocks. **Certain rocks can increase water hardness or contain metals,** which may be detrimental to your aquarium ecosystem. Refer to specific guides to confirm their suitability for aquarium use before adding them to your setup.

A. WOOD

Any wooden elements in the decoration must be prepared before use. One method involves boiling the wood in a 1% diluted bleach solution (suitable for water disinfection) and then letting it dry for one or two weeks in a plastic basin. A few days before placing it in the aquarium, soak it in water to prevent it from floating once in the tank.

However, woods from elm, chestnut, resinous trees, and bark (except cork) are toxic and should be avoided.

B. DECORATED WITH POLYURETHANE FOAM

Decorations made with polyurethane foam are easy to create and carve. However, this material can release toxic substances over time, necessitating thorough hardening with multiple coats of neutral, food-grade epoxy resin. Apply the layers with a brush, allowing an interval of 24 hours between each coat. Sprinkle a layer of dry, clean sand on the last coat of resin before it completely dries.

In the next chapter, we will elaborate on setting up a planted aquarium, particularly those with low requirements—the option we most frequently recommend due to its ease of setup and maintenance.

12 PLANTED AQUARIUM

We aim to provide you with comprehensive information to embark on your journey with a planted aquarium, whether it piques your interest now or in the future. Throughout this book, we've offered insights into key aspects of a planted aquarium. We'd like to emphasize the importance of considering your choice of lighting and substrate right from the start. This way, you can save on costs and avoid any regrets in the future.

In terms of lighting, you can refer back to Chapter 6. To summarize, for **plants with low to medium requirements**, we recommend:

- A white light LED lamp (more cost-effective than colored ones).
- The Chihiros Aquatic Studio brand A series or A plus series could be an excellent choice.
- Lighting **between 25-60 lumens per liter.**
- A color **temperature of 6000-7000 K.**
- **RGBW or RGW** lamps are gaining popularity. Though slightly more expensive, they accentuate the colors of plants and animals, allowing for customization based on your preferences.

Regarding substrate, a summary of our recommendations can be found in Chapter 7. We suggest the following:

- **Avoid using sand** due to its fine granulometry.
- If you're willing to invest a bit more for better results, consider a combination of **volcanic stone + JBL Aquabasis + JBL Manado.**
- For a more budget-friendly option, opt for silica or quartz gravel with a grain size of 1-5 millimeters.
- **Avoid store-bought nutrient substrates with nitrates and phosphates for low to medium-tech aquariums**, especially if you lack experience with their use.
- If you prefer an aquarium planted in nutritious yet **economical substrate**, you can prepare it **yourself using regular terrestrial, universal, plant, or garden substrate.** "Seal" it with at least **2.5-3 cm of inert gravel.**

In terms of water parameters and care for each plant species, we recommend, just as we do for fish, a quick Google search ("care" + (species name)) to gather information on the specific care requirements for each plant you intend to keep. Jot down these details on a sheet for final plant selection. In general, maintaining a **GH between 5 and 20 and a temperature between 20 and 26ºC will provide suitable conditions for most plants.**

In the next section, we'll delve into the various types of planted aquariums based on the plant species, each requiring specific conditions of light, fertilizer, and substrate. For some, this might entail acquiring additional products or equipment like CO2 setups.

12.1 TYPES OF PLANTED AQUARIUMS

Depending on the species of plants that we are going to have in our aquarium, we will need to give them certain conditions of light, fertilizer, and substrate. In some cases, this may mean that we will have to get a new product or equipment in addition to the substrate and lighting, such as CO2 equipment.

LOW OR MEDIUM-TECH AQUARIUMS

"Low-medium tech aquarium"

We are going to show you the **planted aquarium that we recommend** and maintain very frequently. It is characterized by keeping a **small or moderate number of fish, with minimal filtration, cleaning and maintenance** and with a large number of healthy plants and microorganisms. These aquariums are maintained with moderate light and nutrient substrates. Plants with low to medium requirements adapt very easily.

Low-tech aquariums are easier and cheaper to set up and maintain. This is because they take all the advantages of natural processes. For example, bacteria and fish (without administering artificial CO2) provide CO2 to the plants. **The plants help remove ammonium from the water and protect the fish**. And the fish food and substrate provide the plants with nutrients **without adding other fertilizers.** The most common macronutrient deficit we have in this type of aquarium is potassium, but it is not common if we have a nutritious substrate.

Some of the characteristics of these aquariums:

- **They need low maintenance.** It could be maintained for months without water changes (up to 3-6 months or even longer). Only having to replace evaporating water and pruning excess plants.
- **Fish behavior.** A greater number of compatible species and invertebrates will be able to coexist, since the plants will provide them with different areas and shelters. In addition, if the plant species are the usual ones in the regions of the fish, their behavior will be similar to that found in nature.

A. HOW DO PLANTS BENEFIT OUR AQUARIUM?

In aquariums, **both fish and bacteria are continually increasing ammonium levels** as they metabolize food and organic matter. Fortunately, our plants (and algae) prefer ammonium rather than nitrates as their nitrogen source. Folks who have no interest in keeping plants in their aquariums substitute plant labor with frequent water changes, cleaning and vacuuming of gravel or sand, and improving filtration. However, **giving plants a chance can naturally purify the water and lessen the aquarist's efforts.**

1. **They protect fish by removing ammonia (NH_3).** Plants continue to remove ammonium from the water even when they have nitrogen in the substrate or nitrates in the water. This is because **they have a preference for ammonium consumption.**
2. **They protect fish and other animals by removing metals** from the water. Heavy metals may kill them, but they can also inhibit reproduction and appetite. Plants remove metals such as lead, cadmium, copper, zinc and iron from the water.
3. **Algae growth control.** **Good plant growth inhibits algae growth.** How they do this is not clear. However, we do know that they produce a large amount of chemicals that can be toxic to algae. They also **remove iron** from the water, which probably also supports algae control.
4. **Stabilizes pH.** Photosynthesis is an acid-consuming reaction.
5. **They increase the biological activity in the tank.** Many microorganisms (bacteria, protozoa, fungi, algae, etc.) do not live free in the water, but attached to surfaces. Plants, and **especially floating plants, are the ideal home for numerous microorganisms** that recycle nutrients and stabilize the ecosystem of our aquarium.
6. **Oxygenate the water.** Although air probably provides more oxygen to the water than plants (air pumps, filter outlets with Venturi effect, etc.).
7. **They remove CO_2 from the water**. Excess CO_2 (like lack of oxygen) can cause respiratory failure in fish (we may find them gasping at the surface).
8. **They prevent the substrate from becoming toxic.** Plants keep the substrate healthy and it will rarely need to be vacuumed (siphoned).
9. Humic acids from decomposing plants decrease the toxicity of possible heavy metals in the water.

B. FACTORS AFFECTING PLANT GROWTH

We present these factors in the following list:

1. **Nutrients:** Tap water, nutrient substrate, and fish food can supply all the nutrients plants require. **CO_2 is likely the limiting factor** for plant growth in most aquariums. For those with **soft water (GH <4)**, it's essential to note that plants may experience **deficiencies in "hard water nutrients" (Ca, Mg, K, and S).**
2. **Algae Control: Plants cannot grow effectively if algae overwhelm them,** covering their leaves and hindering gas exchange while **consuming available nutrients in the water.**

3. **Fertile Substrates:** In theory, aquatic plants can derive all nutrients from the water. However, in practice, **gravel substrates are not as effective as nutrient substrates. Nutrient-rich substrates provide plants the advantage** they need to flourish and outcompete algae.
4. **Bacteria:** Certain bacteria transform organic matter into CO2 and other nutrients that plants can utilize.
5. **Emergent Plant Growth:** Aquatic plants that have access to air demonstrate better growth compared to those fully submerged. Improved growth enables efficient water filtration.
6. **Adequate Light:** Proper lighting is crucial for plant growth.
7. **Plant Species:** Different plant species may respond differently to your aquarium's conditions (light, substrate, water chemistry, CO2, and even the presence of other plant species). **We recommend incorporating a wide variety of plant species** to enhance your aquarium's likelihood of success. Not all may adapt, but this increases the chances of success.
8. **Nutrient Interactions: An excess of one nutrient can impede the uptake of another.** For instance, an excess of Mn, Zn, or Cu can induce an Fe deficiency in plants, even if there's sufficient Fe in the water.
9. **Moderate Water Movement:** Moderate water movement **benefits plants**, facilitating faster and more efficient transport of CO2 and other nutrients to the leaves. Excessive water flow can reduce photosynthesis, stress the plants mechanically, and potentially remove CO2 from the water through excessive surface movement (though this is negligible and can be offset by using an air pump without issues). For instance, a water movement of 2 cm/sec could be suitable, but you'll refine this with your experience.
10. **Nutrient Uptake Preferences: Plants prefer to absorb phosphate from the substrate via the roots**, while potassium and ammonium are absorbed from the water. Many plant species exhibit a preference for ammonium as a nitrogen source over nitrates. However, high ammonium levels can inhibit growth and prove toxic to animals. Therefore, we do not recommend adding ammonium to aquariums, although some brands include small amounts in their high-tech aquarium fertilizers.

C. HOW TO FERTILIZE A LOW-TECH AQUARIUM?

If your aquarium water is NOT very soft and you use nutrient-rich substrate, **simply ensure your fish are well-fed and minimize cleaning and water changes** to what's necessary. Algae on the crystals should be cleaned as needed. Occasionally, adding **some potassium** is advisable, although this element is typically present in your fish food and substrate and **doesn't require additional fertilization**. Artificial fertilizers are generally only needed for aquariums with artificial CO2 (high-tech) and/or aquariums with very soft water.

Three key takeaways to remember:

1. If your **aquarium is planted** and the fish or other animals do not overcrowd the aquarium, you can **reduce the filter's filtration capacity.**
2. **Very soft waters (GH < 6 - 8) are NOT ideal** for plants due to a deficiency in "hard water nutrients."
3. If your **aquarium water is hard**, note that plants such as "**Foxtail**", "**Elodea**", and "**Vallisneria**" can thrive in your aquarium.

D. CARBON DIOXIDE (CO2) IN OUR AQUARIUM

Lakes and rivers almost always contain more dissolved CO2 in the water than would be expected from equilibrium with the air alone. The additional CO2 is generated by the decomposition of organic matter in the water. Many aquatic plants couldn't survive in nature without this extra CO2 supply. Water in equilibrium with air contains 0.5mg/l CO2, **but many plants require a higher CO2 concentration.**

Determining whether artificial CO2 is worth the **economic cost and the increased difficulty** in handling **is a personal** decision. Generally, **plants grow significantly better with the addition of CO2, as it's often the limiting nutrient**.

However, **artificial CO2 also means investing more time in your aquarium**. For example, if your aquarium water is very soft, you'll likely need to add sodium bicarbonate or calcium carbonate to prevent the water's pH from dropping too low when administering CO2, which could be harmful to the fish.

When artificial CO2 isn't added to the aquarium, CO2 comes from the **decomposition of fish food and organic matter in the substrate**, as well as from the **respiration of the fish**. If you choose this natural method of introducing CO2 into the water, **try to minimize CO2 loss in the aquarium.** Gaseous in nature, CO2 is lost when the water surface is agitated or when "aerators" are used to improve oxygenation. Striking a balance in water surface movement is crucial to ensuring good oxygenation for your fish while minimizing CO2 loss. An excess of CO2 or oxygen deficiency may cause fish to "gasping" at the surface, particularly in the early morning. However, this symptom could have other potential causes. **In practice, there's no clear distinction in using or not using air pumps.** Feel free to use them if needed, especially during warmer seasons.

Here's an illustration of a planted aquarium **with intermediate lighting requirements and NO need for CO2:**

"Medium-tech aquarium"

We leave you a table with the intensity of illumination necessary for each type of plants:

	LOW-TECH	MEDIUM-TECH	HIGH-TECH
LED aquarium	30-40 lm/liter	40-60 lm/liter	>80 lm/liter
Fluorescent aquarium	20 lm/liter	30 lm/liter	>50 lm/liter

Certainly, you **can place plants with low requirements in aquariums with abundant lighting, fertilization, and CO2, but NOT vice versa.** Plants with medium requirements can also be placed in aquariums with low lighting, but keep in mind that their growth may not be optimal, and you won't fully enjoy this type of plants.

B. HIGH-TECH AQUARIUMS

"High-tech aquarium"

High-tech aquariums demand the most resources, both **in terms of equipment** (CO2 system, lighting, fertilizers, substrates, tools, filtration equipment, etc.) **and in terms of time and dedication**. They also entail a significant financial investment, increasing progressively from aquariums without plants, through low-tech aquariums, and peaking with high-tech aquariums.

With the information provided and with the assistance of our colleagues' videos, you'll be able to start with ease and introduce natural plants into your aquarium.

12.2 BASIS FOR SETTING UP A LOW-MEDIUM TECH AQUARIUM

By now, you already possess all the necessary information for setting up this type of aquarium. However, we're going to provide a glimpse of what you'll see in the final chapter. **This is the type of aquarium we often recommend and find the most satisfying. In summary:**

1. **FISH:** Ideally, choose species whose **adult size aligns with the aquarium's capacity**. It's challenging to accommodate larger fish like "oscar" or "Plecostomus" in a home aquarium. For tanks around 40-80 liters, consider species like "Colisa Lalia," small "tetras," "dwarf cichlids," " neons tetra", "cardinal tetra" or "danios." Other species like "angelfish," "loaches," "Congo tetras," and "rainbow" fish could thrive in aquariums of 150 liters or more. **All these mentioned fish are compatible and easy to maintain in a planted aquarium.**

   We strongly **advise against adding new fish to an established aquarium.** Occasionally, a new fish, regardless of its apparent health, can introduce diseases or be disruptive to the existing inhabitants. An alternative is to set up a quarantine aquarium for newly acquired fish. The recommended quarantine period is at least 2 weeks. **Ideally, introducing new fish should be an exception rather than a norm.**

   Treating sick fish, particularly in established or mature tanks, can pose challenges. Antibiotic treatment without a precise diagnosis is often ineffective and potentially harmful to the ecosystem. If treatment is deemed necessary, removing the affected fish to a **separate tank for treatment is ideal.**

2. **LIGHT:** Providing appropriate lighting for a planted aquarium can be perplexing, but the information in the preceding chapters should guide you towards an ideal choice. Regarding direct sunlight, as mentioned earlier, it's advisable to avoid it as it's challenging to control and can promote algae growth while elevating water temperature.

3. **PLANT SELECTION:** Selecting plants that thrive in your aquarium is fundamental to achieving a natural, planted look. Healthy plant growth contributes to water purification, animal protection, and algae control. **Some plants, like Amazon swordfish, thrive better in hard water than in soft water. Planting a variety of species** can help you identify those that suit your aquarium environment. Those that struggle may not survive, while thriving plants will flourish.

   For beginners, it's wise to **avoid high-cost plants like "anubias" and "bucephalandra" initially.** Generally, plants with **higher costs** are challenging to maintain or **have slow growth** rates. On the contrary, **cheaper plants grow rapidly a**nd, under favorable conditions, **can transform your aquarium into a lush garden to enjoy.**

   <u>In conclusion,</u> for beginners or those attempting a planted aquarium, **opting for a variety of affordable plant species and determining which ones thrive best in your specific aquarium is advisable.**

Basic maintenance tips:

a. **Feeding:** Clear indicators of <u>overfeeding</u> include cloudy or foul-smelling water and leftover food on the bottom the following day.
b. **Water Changes:** <u>Well-established aquariums require infrequent water changes</u>. In a well-planted, mature aquarium, a <u>25-30% change every 3-6 months</u>, unless issues arise, should suffice.
c. **Gravel Cleaning:** In planted aquariums, <u>gravel cleaning is unnecessary as it inhibits the renewal of consumed nutrients</u>. Healthy plants rooted in the substrate eliminate the need for gravel cleaning.
d. **Filters and Water Movement:** <u>Moderate water movement</u> aids in nutrient delivery to plants, oxygenation for fish and bacteria, and even heat distribution. Excessive filtration may not be beneficial for well-planted aquariums

Here is a list of easy-care aquarium plants for your convenience:

- **Slow Growth:** Java Fern (Microsorum pteropus), Anubias (Anubias spp.), Java Moss (Taxiphyllum barbieri), Cryptocoryne (Cryptocoryne spp.)

- **Fast Growth:** Hornwort (Ceratophyllum demersum), Vallisneria (Vallisneria spp.), Elodea najas, Ambulia (Limnophila sessiliflora), Hygrophila (Hygrophila spp.).

- **Floating Plants:** Duckweed (Lemna minor), Water Spangles (Salvinia natans), Amazon Frogbit (Limnobium laevigatum)

Perfect for any aquarium, these plants are hardy and can tolerate a wide range of water conditions. None require advanced gardening skills. They offer aesthetic benefits and contribute to the balance of the ecosystem in your aquarium. **Many other plants exist that we haven't mentioned.** You can easily find more information about them on the internet, and they are readily available in almost any aquarium store.

13 THE END OF ALGAE

This will be a concise yet significant chapter, **addressing one of the most prevalent concerns for hobbyists in aquarium maintenance—the unwanted growth of algae.** It often proves frustrating and could lead to aquarists giving up on maintaining plants in their tanks.

"High-tech aquarium with green filamentous algae"

13.1 COMMON METHODS TO COMBAT AND CONTROL ALGAE IN LITERATURE

- **Algaecides and Antibiotics:** Algaecides are chemicals designed to eradicate algae but can often cause more harm than good in planted aquariums. Copper and simazine are common components of algaecides, both of which are toxic to fish and plants. Determining the proper dosage to eliminate algae without harming plants and fish is highly challenging. Additionally, when algae die off, they release toxins, and it is not uncommon for the abrupt death of algae to harm our animals.

    Regarding antibiotics, it appears that cyanobacteria can be eliminated with antibiotics such as erythromycin. However, sometimes, following the initial treatment, bacteria can develop resistance, and higher doses may harm the plants. Our aquarium functions as an ecosystem and reacts poorly to toxins or antibiotics. Even if effective initially, the problem is highly likely to recur.

- **Reduced Light Period:** Algae are akin to submerged plants and can utilize only a fraction of sunlight, being adversely affected by light intensity. Most algae thrive in low light conditions. The mechanism by which plants appear to flourish in sunlight may be related to iron, as sunlight boosts iron availability to plants. <u>If we cover the aquarium to block light, we will also harm our plants.</u>

- **Water Changes:** Many hobbyists report that they have been unable to control algae with water changes. Additionally, we have provided reasons why excessively frequent water changes in the aquarium may be detrimental.

- **Fish, Shrimp, and Snails:** <u>These organisms can be useful</u> in controlling algae. <u>Snails also aid in cleaning plant leaves.</u> Some species of snails consume decaying plant parts (we recommend "physas" and "planorbis", which are readily available and inexpensive). However, relying solely on these animals for algae control can be counterproductive in the long run. They tend to consume the algae they prefer, and it's only a matter of time before some types of algae they don't like to eat appear. For example, we are not aware of any aquarium fish species that enjoy consuming cyanobacteria.

- **Phosphate Removal:** It is widely accepted that phosphate limits algal growth in freshwater. Phosphate concentrations in unpolluted natural water are very low, ranging between 0.003 and 0.02 mg/l P. Many algae species cannot grow below 0.02 mg/L of phosphate. However, <u>our aquariums typically have much higher phosphate levels</u> (1-5mg/L or more). <u>Phosphate is continuously introduced through fish food, making it challenging to control algae growth</u> by attempting to regulate phosphate levels.

The truth is that, in well-established aquariums with plants, significant algae problems are rare. We will delve into the reasons for this shortly.

13.2 COMPETITION BETWEEN ALGAE AND PLANTS

Algae typically excel in utilizing light and nutrients more efficiently than plants. Nevertheless, there are encouraging studies showcasing the reduction of algae population, from 6,600 cells/ml to 430 cells/ml, by adding "Elodea" to ponds.

A. ADVANTAGES OF <u>ALGAE OVER PLANTS</u>

- **Better adaptation to low light:** Aquatic plants usually have higher light requirements than many algae.
- **Better adaptation to the light spectrum:** While plants and green algae have chlorophyll that predominantly absorbs red and blue light, many algae possess accessory photosynthetic pigments enabling them to utilize the entire light spectrum effectively.
- **Better adaptation to high pH:** Some plants, especially those capable of utilizing bicarbonate as a carbon source in addition to CO2, compete better with algae in high pH conditions. Examples include "Vallisneria," "Foxtail," and "Elodea."
- **Better nutrient uptake from water:** Certain algae species are more adept at nutrient absorption from water than plants. While plants struggle to grow with phosphates at 0.075mg/L, some algae can readily consume these phosphates.
- **Greater species diversity:** An aquarium will only have the plant species intentionally introduced, which might not adapt well to tank conditions. On the contrary, algae can enter the aquarium through various means like fish, plants, substrates, and airborne spores.

B. ADVANTAGES OF PLANTS OVER ALGAE

- **Roots:** Plants can extract nutrients from the substrate and are not solely reliant on nutrients from the water.
- **Emergent plants:** These plants can utilize light to its full intensity and absorb CO2 from the air, overcoming limitations on carbon use, similar to submerged plants.
- **Nutrient reserves:** Plants can utilize nutrient reserves even when temperature, light, and nutrient conditions are less than ideal.

"Low-tech aquarium with homemade substrate, requiring minimal maintenance, without CO2 injection, and algae-free"

13.3 FACTORS INFLUENCING ALGAE CONTROL

Considering the above, the following factors should be taken into account:

- **Emergent and floating plants:** These plants grow much faster than fully submerged ones, resulting in increased nutrient consumption in the aquarium, potentially stimulating algae growth. They can also help reduce excess light that submerged plants do not need, potentially protecting them from algae. Instead of reducing light intensity, it might be advisable to maintain a moderate intensity and add floating plants to encourage emergent growth of submerged plants.
- **Iron:** Iron could be the limiting nutrient for algae growth in our aquariums, given that other nutrients like nitrate and phosphate are abundant. This is why issues might arise when setting up aquariums with potting

or garden substrate, as a significant amount of iron might be released into the water during the first 2 months. After this period, problems tend to diminish. Plants will continue to extract iron from the substrate, but algae rely solely on the free iron in the water. Remember, it's essential to cover the potting medium with at least 2.5 cm of gravel.

- **Allelopathy:** Plants release chemicals into the water that can partially inhibit algal growth. Conversely, algae could also release these chemicals and inhibit plant growth.

- **Appearance of new algae species:** Within our aquariums, a delicate balance exists between plants and algae. Occasionally, in mature aquariums with well-growing plants and no prior issues, a new algae species might unexpectedly appear and cover the entire tank. While this is an exceptional occurrence, it's likely that there's an imbalance in the ecosystem that we have not yet identified.

There are numerous variables in caring for a particular aquarium and potential problems that can arise. It would be impossible to cover them all in one book. But if we take into account the small tips we are seeing, it is very likely that we won't have to face many of them. And when they do appear, with these tools, you will be able to solve them!

A mature aquarium is a complex ecosystem. Even if one tank is set up identically to another, it will undoubtedly develop its own unique characteristics over time. All we can do is set up an aquarium, **follow the advice provided, and hope it develops along the desired path.** *If done correctly, we can likely prevent many problems from occurring.*

14 THE INHABITANTS OF THE AQUARIUM

Selecting the right animals is a critical aspect of creating a thriving ecosystem. Each species has specific water requirements and care needs. Some have a broad range of ideal parameters, while others may be more limited.

If we compare the time devoted to choosing our fish, shrimp, and invertebrates with the effort invested in other aspects of the project, it's relatively small.

To give you an idea, dedicating just two hours can help you compile a list of preferred species, review their care requirements and ideal conditions, and decide which ones are best suited for your ecosystem. Consider factors such as water parameters (GH or ppm), temperature, etc., as well as the ideal decoration. **This investment of time is minimal but can save you considerable inconvenience in the future.**

"Community aquarium"

As discussed in the early sections of this book about selecting an aquarium, **there are two primary approaches:**

1. **Setting up a specific aquarium:** When you have a particular species or group of species in mind and want to create an aquarium tailored to them. For instance, "I want to set up a Lake Tanganyika biotope aquarium."

2. **Choosing the right species for your ideal aquarium:** <u>This is more common among beginners in aquarium keeping.</u> You choose the tank volume and other equipment based on space available, budget, time constraints, and personal preferences. The question then is: <u>How do you select the species and determine the number of fish for your aquarium?</u>

In the first case, this book equips you with the fundamentals to establish the basis of your ecosystem. From there, you'll need to delve into the specific species of animals you've chosen: their care, ideal conditions, etc., and adapt the equipment accordingly if needed. Below, you'll find a list outlining the "Most relevant aspects of each species in terms of care and habitat," which will be invaluable for adjusting your ecosystem.

In the second case, where you've already decided on the tank and other equipment, we'll guide you on how to choose the ideal fish for your aquarium:

14.1 HOW TO CHOOSE THE SPECIES AND NUMBER OF FISH?

HOW TO RESEARCH FISH SPECIES FROM THE START?

- Conduct online research: Look for guides on fish compatibility, beginner-friendly fish, fish guides for small or large aquariums, etc., and review them.
- Explore local sources: Check your country's websites to discover the species available. For example, in Spain, you can find information at www.dnatecosistemas.es, which covers nearly all available species.
- Visualize: Look at pictures and videos of aquariums, and specific species to understand their behavior.
- **Create a list: Jot down the names of the species you find most appealing.**

We discourage shipping fish by parcel, although unfortunately, this is a common method to transport them to stores. We believe that this practice should be avoided whenever possible.

Once you've compiled a list of 5, 10, or 15 species, research each one on Google by searching "fish care + (species name)." Compare the information from at least two different sources. Focus on the following characteristics:

MOST RELEVANT ASPECTS OF EACH FISH SPECIES IN TERMS OF CARE AND HABITAT

- **Minimum recommended aquarium volume** for the species.
- Approximate **adult size** of the specimen.
- Ideal water conditions and parameter range: **GH, temperature,** etc.
- **Diet** and nutrition.
- **Behavior and compatibility:** Are they calm or active fish? Are they suitable for community aquariums? Do they thrive in groups or schools? What's the recommended group size? Are they territorial?
- Preferred swimming level in the aquarium: Do they stay at the bottom, surface, or mid-level?
- **Recommended decorative elements**: Natural plants, hiding spots, amount of open space without decoration?
- **Reproduction** details (for those interested in breeding fish).

By doing this, you can eliminate fish species and narrow down your **selection to a maximum of 3-4 species, suitable for a 100-liter aquarium**. For a 60–70-liter aquarium, 2-3 fish species may be sufficient. Keep in mind that **many species live in groups or schools.** Separating them can cause stress, hiding, poor feeding, and compromised health.

Additionally, consider where the fish swim within the aquarium—whether at the surface, mid-level, or bottom. It's ideal to maintain a balance in the different levels of the tank to avoid overcrowding any particular level.

The fact that a fish is territorial within its species does not necessarily mean it will show the same behavior towards other species. Delve deeper into these aspects based on your interests.

<u>And most importantly,</u> resist the temptation to overcrowd your aquarium!

14.2 HOW MANY FISH CAN YOU HAVE ACCORDING TO THE SIZE OF YOUR TANK?

As a general guideline, it's advisable to provide **one liter of water for every centimeter of fish**. This rule works well for many small tropical fish, such as tetras, rasboras, guppies, platies, some rainbow fish, and so on.

In practice, however, we often tend to overcrowd our aquariums. For instance, **in a 60-liter aquarium**, an ideal population might consist of **around 15-20 fish, each measuring about 3-4 cm.**

Throughout this book, we've emphasized the importance of investing a bit more in filtration equipment or opting for aquariums with natural plants. One reason for this recommendation is the common occurrence of overpopulation in aquariums.

However, **fish size isn't the sole factor determining the appropriate fish population for your tank.**

FACTORS TO CONSIDER

- **1 cm of fish for every liter isn't an absolute rule.** Fish like discus or goldfish, for instance, require 30-40 liters of water for each adult specimen. You'll find similar recommendations in care sheets for each fish.
- **The filtration capacity of your aquarium matters**. A higher flow rate, sufficient filter media, and good quality filter media allow for a larger fish population.
- **The presence of plants also plays a role.** More plants provide hiding spots, reduce stress in crowded tanks, and help lower nitrate concentrations.
- **Consider other tank inhabitants**, like small invertebrates (snails, shrimps), as they contribute to debris and organic material levels in the tank.
- **The frequency of water changes and bottom cleaning**. More fish mean faster nitrate buildup, necessitating more frequent maintenance.

Remember to consider the adult size of the fish when making these calculations.

Here's another essential tip: to minimize disease risk, avoid introducing fish or other organisms from other aquariums. Initially, this might be challenging, so selecting a reputable store for purchasing animals and plants is crucial. You can also seek fish from fellow aquarium hobbyists. Ensure the store maintains clean aquariums without sick animals, and inquire about quarantining procedures for new arrivals or sick animals.

For those with the option of a second tank, quarantining new fish for two weeks before introducing them to the main aquarium is a viable strategy.

WHERE TO GET YOUR FISH?

Finding a trustworthy store is key, noted for their **well-maintained ecosystems and healthy fish**. This significantly reduces the likelihood of introducing fish with transmissible diseases into your aquarium.

Another avenue is sourcing fish from fellow hobbyists, but be vigilant about the health of their aquariums and fish before integrating them into your setup.

"Red Cherry Neocaridina"

INTRODUCING FISH TO THE AQUARIUM

The introduction of fish and other animals into your aquarium for the first time is a crucial process to ensure the health and well-being of your aquatic inhabitants while maintaining the ecosystem's stability. Exercise patience and follow these straightforward steps:

<u>General Recommendations</u>

1. **Acclimatization**: When you arrive home with the fish, it is essential to acclimate them to reduce stress. Turn off the aquarium lights and float the sealed bag on the water's surface for about 15-20 minutes to match the water temperature in the bag with that of the aquarium.
2. Open the bag after 5-10 minutes and begin **adding aquarium water in small quantities at regular intervals of 10-15 minutes.**
3. Continue this process for **at least 1 hour until at least 2/3 of the water in the bag is from your aquarium.**

4. Afterward, release the fish carefully. Use a net to gently transfer the fish from the bag to the aquarium. **Do not pour the bag water into the aquarium**, as it may contain pathogenic microorganisms or algae.

For invertebrates, such as shrimp, the acclimatization process is similar to that of fish. However, they have a **lower tolerance for changes**. Begin adding aquarium water in even **smaller quantities**, and the process of adding aquarium water should last **at least 2 hours in this case.**

Remember that introducing new inhabitants should be done with caution and patience. Conduct research on the specific requirements of the species you wish to introduce and follow the proper steps to ensure they adapt smoothly to their new habitat."

We've poured our enthusiasm and dedication into creating this book, hoping to enhance your enjoyment of this hobby. We trust you've discovered what you were seeking.

See you next time!

APPENDIX 1. CHEMICAL FILTRATION

Chemical filtration can be utilized to modify specific water parameters or the concentration of certain compounds. There is a wide variety of products, each with its own distinct functions and properties. These are employed to optimize water conditions in very precise cases.

Remember: DO NOT use chemical filtration materials that remove nitrates or organic matter from the aquarium during the cycling process; it will delay cycling. Additionally, most of these methods cannot be used permanently in planted aquariums.

APPLICATIONS OF CHEMICAL FILTRATION

- To remove nitrogen compounds, by-products of organic matter degradation (nitrate, nitrites, ammonium...) and also phosphates:
    - **Permanent use:** In non-planted aquariums, to reduce the need for water changes and limit algae growth.
    - **Occasional use:** For example, to address green water caused by unicellular algae by removing the nutrients they utilize and retaining some of these unicellular algae.
    - Modify pH.

- Eliminating residual medication after a treatment.
- Eliminate unpleasant odors.
- Eliminate tannins released by wood if clear water is preferred.

The chemical media should be placed last in the water flow within our filter, following biological filtration.

Activated carbon has always been the standard filtering material, readily available, cost-effective, and highly functional. However, other options have emerged, such as **synthetic adsorbent resins**, offering advantages over activated carbon: they can be used for specific purposes like adsorbing and reducing phosphate concentration in water (as a preventive measure against algae), adsorbing calcium and magnesium ions to lower water hardness, or adsorbing nitrogen compounds. Some of these synthetic resins **do NOT have a "rebound effect":** once they have removed the compounds from the water, they will not reintroduce them when saturated, unlike activated carbon.

On the other hand, acidifying peats introduce tannic and humic acids into the water, lowering the pH of the aquarium.

SOME CHEMICAL FILTER MEDIA

A. ACTIVATED CARBON FOR AQUARIUM

Store it hermetically sealed, as it can absorb substances from the air. **It cannot be reused once saturated**. When placing it in the aquarium filter, encase it in a stocking or another fine-mesh material.

It's crucial to purchase **activated carbon suitable for aquarium use**, as some may be cheaper but potentially toxic.

Activated carbon **can be used to reduce nitrate, nitrite, ammonium, and phosphate levels, as well as to remove certain medications from the water**. Generally, 24-48 hours of use should suffice to remove a medication from the water. For addressing an algae issue, using it temporarily for 7-10 days (while resolving the source of the problem) should be adequate.

Remember that when this material becomes saturated, it starts releasing the compounds it had previously removed back into the water.

B. ACIDIFYING PEATS

Acidifying peats introduce various substances into the water to lower the pH. They tint the water due to the tannic and humic acids they release, resembling the natural color of the water in certain fish habitats like "killifish" and others of Amazonian origin. They can be used for **specific biotopes** or to condition the water for species that require a lower pH.

WHY NOT USE CHEMICAL FILTER MEDIA WIDELY?

- **Costs:** Around 15 euros for each product, with a quantity sufficient to treat 100-200 liters for 1 year.
- While they may provide advantages in the long run, **initially**, they can **complicate aquarium management**. It's an additional technique that requires learning and an investment of time.
- They necessitate **larger filtration equipment** or an extra filter.
- Their use is discretionary; if you follow the advice in this guide, you can maintain a healthy aquarium with ideal water without resorting to additional products.
- Permanent use is only feasible in aquariums without plants.

SYNTHETIC ADSORBENT RESINS

Let's discuss two particularly useful products. One is **a resin that absorbs nitrogenous compounds** such as ammonia, nitrites, and nitrates, while the **other removes phosphates from the water**. Utilizing a combination of both in a planted aquarium can be an effective method to deter algae and reduce the frequency of water changes.

There are also **decalcifying resins** that absorb calcium carbonate and magnesium from the aquarium, reducing the GH of the water. However, **their use is entirely unnecessary** if you prepare the water as we have explained, which is simpler and more cost-effective.

A. SEACHEM PURIGEN

Seachem Purigen contains a synthetic macro-porous polymer that effectively removes nitrogenous compounds such as ammonia, nitrite, and nitrate from the water. Its impact on other compounds is minimal.

It can be regenerated by treating it with chlorine (bleach) once it is exhausted. A 100 ml bag of Purigen can treat up to 400 liters of water for 6 months.

The cost of a 100ml bag is approximately 15 euros.

B. SEACHEM PHOSGUARD

Seachem PhosGuard is designed to remove phosphate and silicate from water. A 100 ml bag of this product can treat up to 120 liters for 6 months, depending on the concentration of phosphate and silicate in the water. Importantly, PhosGuard is not an exchange resin and does not release any substances into the water.

PhosGuard does not reintroduce phosphates or silicates back into the water (similar to Purigen), and it can be removed, dried, and reused until exhausted.

The cost of a 250ml bag is approximately 15 euros.

AN EXAMPLE OF HOW TO USE CHEMICAL FILTRATION

Our recommendation for employing chemical filtration **is to use it in non-planted aquariums with the goal of reducing phosphates and nitrates to 0.** This approach helps minimize the risk of algae growth in the aquarium, maintain excellent water quality free of these toxins for our aquatic inhabitants, and extend maintenance intervals for tasks like water changes, algae cleaning, and glass maintenance.

However, there are considerations to bear in mind. We need to be vigilant about replacing the filtration material once it becomes saturated.

Remember, the primary and most crucial aspect of filtration is biological filtration. If space permits, a thin layer of mechanical filtration using a foam sponge can be added, followed by the consideration of incorporating chemical filtration in any available compartments. It's crucial to position chemical filtration after the biological layer and as the final step before the water exits the filter. After placing all the filtering material, ensure that the water flow isn't significantly impeded; having an excess of filtering material is pointless if water doesn't pass through it effectively.

If your current filter doesn't meet these conditions, you may need to acquire a second filter for chemical filtration or opt not to use chemical filtration.

We recommend starting with two products, although there are many others with similar characteristics:

- **SEACHEM PHOSGUARD** - 250ML (14 euros). Use 100mL per 120 liters of water in the aquarium, with about 6 months of effectiveness. Not reusable. Removes phosphates and silicates from the water.
- **SEACHEM PURIGEN** - 100ML (15 euros). A 100 ml bag of Purigen treats up to 400 liters of water for six months. It is reusable. It removes organic matter before it transforms into nitrate, i.e., it does not remove nitrate from the water.

These products are relatively simple to use, with detailed instructions provided. You can also find helpful tutorials on YouTube and blogs where fellow aquarists share their experiences. It's essential to cross-reference information since misinformation is widespread, and selecting reliable sources is paramount.

THE FOURTH METHOD FOR LOWERING NITRATES

In addition to weekly water changes, implementing general measures to reduce nitrate production (such as having plants, maintaining a balanced animal population, and avoiding overfeeding), and employing chemical filtration, there's another method previously mentioned in the filtration chapter. However, its impact on nitrate reduction is not as significant as the earlier recommendations.

We mentioned earlier that nitrifying bacteria are aerobic and require oxygen to survive, but **there are also anaerobic bacteria that can remove nitrates and cannot coexist with oxygen.** Biological filter materials are often porous, and some, like "**De Nitrate by Seachem,**" possess high porosity, enabling anaerobic conditions (absence of oxygen) and aiding in the removal of nitrates from the water.

Although this method of nitrate removal isn't as prominent, it's worth considering. It's a slow process that requires specific conditions in our aquariums (as indicated in the manufacturer's usage instructions), and it's not a sole solution but can complement other methods.

"**Seachem's "Matrix"** is also highly porous and may possess the capability to reduce nitrates. This might also apply to **"Pure by Neo Media."**

For both "Matrix" and "Denitrate" by Seachem, you can find usage instructions on Google, and it's crucial to review them before making a purchase. For instance, "Denitrate" is not recommended for filters with a high-water flow rate. **To purchase any of these products, simply search the product name followed by "buy" on Google to find the most cost-effective option.**

APPENDIX 2. EXAMPLES AND BUDGETS OF COMPLETE EQUIPMENT

We've curated two examples to demonstrate how to select a complete setup based on the information provided in this book:

EXAMPLE 1. "THE GOLDFISH TANK".

This setup is suitable for a 200-liter aquarium, designed for goldfish or any freshwater fish species that don't require many hiding places, like cichlids or discus. While each species may have specific needs, the fundamental equipment remains consistent.

"Goldfish aquarium"

In summary, this setup entails a 200-liter aquarium equipped with external filtration, LED lighting, and a silica sand-based substrate. We will examine each component separately, highlighting those that are essential and recommended, as well as optional ones depending on the circumstances:

ESSENTIAL AND RECOMMENDED EQUIPMENT

THE TANK

We opted for a custom-made tank without a lid, featuring "optical" front glass for superior transparency. The dimensions are 100 cm (length) x 40 cm (width) x 50 cm (height). If you reside in Spain and buy from "Aquariums Hispania":

Price: 170 euros.

Search for custom aquarium stores in your region and compare prices for the best deal.

THE FILTER

Eheim Professionel Pro 4 350+: with a flow rate of 1050 liters/hour and 5 liters capacity for filter material. The inlet and outlet hose diameters are 16 mm (inner diameter) and 22 mm (outer diameter).

The filter comes with all necessary filter material and equipment to start.

Price: 170 euros.

LIGHTING

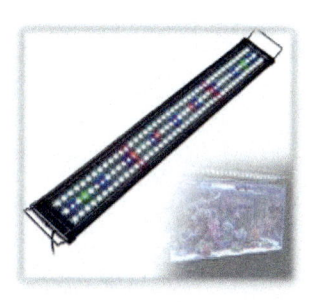

One LED lamp with 5 colors suitable for aquariums measuring 100-105 cm. Power: 23W and 5418lm lumens. Available on AliExpress.

Price: 38 euros.

SUBSTRATE

AXTON 25 kg bag of silica sand from Leroy Merlin. If this brand is unavailable, look for similar options in your region (as explained in the substrate section).

Price: 5 euros.

TDS METER

Available for purchase at various stores, including AliExpress.

Price: 7 euros.

THERMOMETER

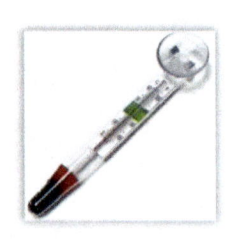

A basic thermometer.

Price: 1 euro on AliExpress

BACTERIA FOR CYCLING (RECOMMENDED)

Azoo Plus Ultrabioguard or Microbe-Lift Special Blend. We recommend either of these two brands, both delivering similar results. Prioritize being well-informed before making a purchase.

Price: 20 euros.

POWER STRIPS, SOCKETS AND TIMERS

Two options: a power strip with a WiFi controller featuring at least 4-6 sockets or a power strip with a minimum of 4-6 outlets and at least 2 timers. The price on AliExpress is consistent for both options.

Price: 20 euros.

AERATOR (RECOMMENDED).

The recommended aerator from the corresponding chapter is likely sufficient for this 200-liter aquarium. Alternatively, you can find aerators on AliExpress for 8 euros. Horizontal tubes to create columns of bubbles are also available.

Price: 10 euros.

TOTAL COST OF EQUIPMENT FOR A 200 LITER AQUARIUM

Considering the equipment, the value for money is great:

441 euros

TOTAL COST OF EQUIPMENT FOR A 100-LITER AQUARIUM

An aquarium of similar characteristics, but with a tank **of 100 liters**, a **Seachem Tidal 110** filter and a similar lamp adapted to the size of the tank and without modifying the rest of the equipment, cost:

226 euros

In general, the budget for aquariums of similar characteristics, whether planted or not, nearly doubles when the tank's volume is doubled.

OPTIONAL/CIRCUMSTANTIAL EQUIPMENT

HEATER (CIRCUMSTANTIAL)

The heater is only optional if you are setting up a cold-water aquarium.

Price: 8-10 euros (AliExpress).

FAN (CIRCUMSTANTIAL)

In warm regions, especially during summer, consider a fan if the water temperature exceeds 28°C, especially 30°C.

Price: 25 euros (AliExpress).

TRANSPARENT GLASS WATER INLET AND OUTLET (OPTIONAL)

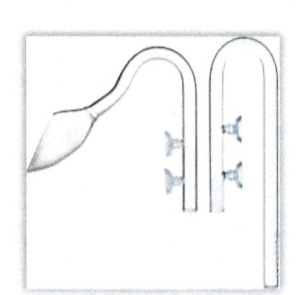

These elegant accessories, designed for external filters, are available on AliExpress in various sizes to match filter tubes' thickness.

Price: 16 euros (for both)

PRE-FILTER (OPTIONAL/CIRCUMSTANCE)

Price: 1 euro (4 units on AliExpress).

Also, there are cylindrical filters with a metal grid, which are even better than those with a sponge.

EXAMPLE 2. "MY WATER GARDEN".

This is an aquascaping aquarium. In this case, although its size is small (as per the criteria), we could classify it as a Dutch-type aquascape, where the main theme is plants. It's a more complex setup than the previous one, requiring more skills, knowledge, attention, and maintenance time from your part.

We opted for a smaller aquarium to create a significant contrast in terms of equipment and costs compared to the 200-liter example.

"High-tech planted aquarium"

In summary, it's a 45-liter aquarium equipped with a backpack filtration system, powerful LED lighting, a combined substrate of JBL Manado, a CO2 system, and daily fertilizers. We will review each component separately, highlighting the essentials and recommendations, and discussing optional elements based on individual cases:

ESSENTIAL AND RECOMMENDED EQUIPMENT

THE TANK

We've chosen a custom-made aquarium without a lid, featuring an "optical" front glass to enhance visibility. Its dimensions are 50 cm (length) x 30 cm (width) x 30 cm (height). If you're in Spain, you can purchase it from "Aquariums Hispania."

Price: 48 euros.

THE FILTER

We recommend the Tidal 75 by Seachem, a slightly oversized filter considering the aquarium's dimensions. The ample decomposition of organic matter from plants will produce significant ammonium amounts, affecting the flow in the filter. The filter comes with all necessary filtering materials and startup equipment.

Price: 60-70 euros.

LIGHTING

Opt for a Chihiro's LED lamp with a controller and 4 color LEDs (red, blue, green, and white). Suitable for aquariums of 45-60 cm. It offers a power of 49W and 3600lm lumens. Available on AliExpress.

Price: 135 euros.

SUBSTRATE

For the substrate, we recommend a combination of JBL Manado, JBL Aquabasis, and volcanic stone, as detailed in the substrate chapter.

Price: 30 euros.

A homemade nutrient-rich substrate for terrestrial plants can indeed be a viable and cost-effective option

TDS METER (Price: 7 euros) + **THERMOMETER (Price: 1 euro on AliExpress)** + **BACTERIES FOR CYCLING (RECOMMENDED) (Price: 20 euros)** + **POWER STRIPS, SOCKETS, AND TIMERS** (Price: 20 euros) + **AIR BLOWER (RECOMMENDED)** (Price: 15 euros) + **FERTILIZER** (Price: 8 euros)

TEST FOR WATER

In the best case and following our recommendation to buy only the nitrate and phosphate test:

Price: 40 euros.

CO2 BOTTLE

A second-hand CO2 cylinder from a fire extinguisher company costs 20 euros in Spain.

Price: 20 euros.

CO2 REGULATOR

AliExpress. **Price: 30 euros.**

DIFFUSER

AliExpress. **Price: 10 euros.**

TOOLS FOR PLANTED AQUARIUMS

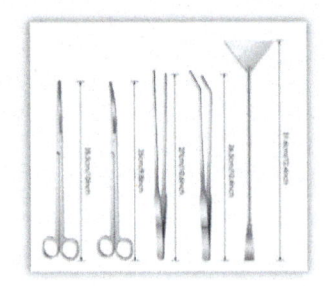

AliExpress. **Price: 15 euros.**

HEATER

We need the water to be at least above 18ºC for our plants.

Price: 10 euros (AliExpress).

TOTAL COST OF EQUIPMENT FOR A 50 LITER AQUARIUM

Typically, the costs for a planted aquarium are higher. At "Mejor Acuario", we've put effort into finding the best techniques and quality equipment at reasonable prices.

460 euros

TOTAL COST OF EQUIPMENT FOR A 90 LITER AQUARIUM

For a similar aquarium with a 90-liter tank, an Eheim Pro 4 250 filter, and a lamp adjusted to the tank's size while increasing the substrate, the total cost would be:

690 euros

If you enjoyed the book, please share your experience by leaving a positive comment on Amazon! Your opinion is crucial to us and to other aquarium enthusiasts. Thank you for being a part of our community!

Do not hesitate to contact us!
See you next time!

On Facebook: https://www.facebook.com/Mejor-Acuario-100153475359250
And on Instagram: https://www.instagram.com/mejor_acuario/

Alejandro Sánchez Martínez

"Mejor Acuario", Spain.

Printed in Great Britain
by Amazon